NORTH AYRSHIRE

D0229052

Also by John Stammers

The Picador Book of

Love Poems

The Picador Book of
Love Poems

EDITED BY

John Stammers

PICADOR

First published 2011 by Picador
an imprint of Pan Macmillan, a division of Macmillan Publishers Limited
Pan Macmillan, 20 New Wharf Road, London N1 9RR
Basingstoke and Oxford
Associated companies throughout the world
www.panmacmillan.com

ISBN 978-0-330-50902-2

Copyright © John Stammers 2011

The right of John Stammers to be identified as the
editor of this work has been asserted by him in accordance
with the Copyright, Designs and Patents Act 1988.

Every effort has been made to contact copyright holders of material
reproduced in this book. If any have been inadvertently overlooked, the publishers
will be pleased to make restitution at the earliest opportunity.

The acknowledgements on pages 175–6 constitute an extension of
this copyright page.

All rights reserved. No part of this publication may be
reproduced, stored in or introduced into a retrieval system, or
transmitted, in any form, or by any means (electronic, mechanical,
photocopying, recording or otherwise) without the prior written
permission of the publisher. Any person who does any unauthorized
act in relation to this publication may be liable to criminal
prosecution and civil claims for damages.

1 3 5 7 9 8 6 4 2

A CIP catalogue record for this book is available from
the British Library.

Printed in the UK by CPI Mackays, Chatham ME5 8TD

Visit www.picador.com to read more about all our books
and to buy them. You will also find features, author interviews and
news of any author events, and you can sign up for e-newsletters
so that you're always first to hear about our new releases.

for Isolde

NORTH AYRSHIRE LIBRARIES	
05806453	
Bertrams	18/02/2011
808.8	£12.99
L	

Song of Solomon 2:1, The Rose of Sharon

I am the rose of Sharon, and the lily of the valleys. As the lily among thorns, so is my love among the daughters. As the apple tree among the trees of the wood, so is my beloved among the sons. I sat down under his shadow with great delight, and his fruit was sweet to my taste. He brought me to the banqueting house, and his banner over me was love.

Stay me with flagons, comfort me with apples: for I am sick of love. His left hand is under my head, and his right hand doth embrace me. I charge you, O ye daughters of Jerusalem, by the roes, and by the hinds of the field, that ye stir not up, nor awake my love, till he please. The voice of my beloved! behold, he cometh leaping upon the mountains, skipping upon the hills. My beloved is like a roe or a young hart: behold, he standeth behind our wall, he looketh forth at the windows, shewing himself through the lattice. My beloved spake, and said unto me, Rise up, my love, my fair one, and come away.

For, lo, the winter is past, the rain is over and gone; The flowers appear on the earth; the time of the singing of birds is come, and the voice of the turtle is heard in our land.

The fig tree putteth forth her green figs, and the vines with the tender grape give a good smell. Arise, my love, my fair one, and come away. O my dove, that art in the clefts of the rock, in the secret places of the stairs, let me see thy countenance, let me hear thy voice; for sweet is thy voice, and thy countenance is comely. Take us the foxes, the little foxes, that spoil the vines: for our vines have tender grapes. My beloved is mine, and I am his: he feedeth among the lilies. Until the day break, and the shadows flee away, turn, my beloved, and be thou like a roe or a young hart upon the mountains of Bether.

Contents

xi

xii

Introduction

The poetry of love is unlike any other. No other poetry has its singularity of focus. It is the dominant theme of most Western poetry since the Renaissance, and in English poetry finds its most characteristic and celebrated expression, from the sonnets of Shakespeare to the movie-derived notoriety of Auden's clocks. This is the love of one person for another, typified, if not necessarily defined, by erotic desire, its sources and its various consequences. This variety may or may not have been exhausted by poets over the centuries, but love's aspects are certainly numerous: attraction, courtship, disappointment, consummation, betrayal, loss and regret are all themes that run multiple threads through the fabric of our love poetry.

In making the selection for this anthology, I have drawn as widely as possible from all those themes. On some occasions this has meant calling in as witness love's fleshy associate, sex; on others, its social one, marriage; and once or twice its legal one, divorce.

I was also keen to include a considerable number of modern and contemporary poems. I was also determined that I would include all the poems from the past that I considered canonical. That said, I limited myself mainly to poems written in English and since the Renaissance – the one exception being *The Rose of Sharon* from the Song of Solomon, which I felt was a kind of original touchstone. I've made this what I believe to be the anthology's appropriate epigraph.

During the process of simultaneously reading poems of the past and of the present, it became clear that an exchange was taking place. A striking feature of poetry as an art form is that it has an intimate involvement with its own history: that's to say that poets treat poems from the canon not as dead artefacts, but as living texts, to be re-examined and engaged with. This practice of poetic allusion is more than simply a quoting of earlier works: it's a dynamic process, a dialogue between not just poets but the poems themselves. One of the things that provides poetry with its lasting power is just this inter-weaving, a kind of cultural density; and nowhere is this more true in the poetry of love.

It seemed to me that this dialogue reflected something like the conversational, two-way nature of romantic love itself. I realized one way of presenting the poems was as a set of pairs, of couples: one from the canon, followed by one from a modern or contemporary poet. These might be directly linked, or they might deal with the same issue – whether or not in a similar way. (The one exception to this arrange-ment is the pair of poems by the two Brownings, which I couldn't bear to put asunder. I've placed them at the centre of the book, where I hope they form a unique reference point of a historically real, enduring love between two great poets.)

As Shakespeare demonstrated so effectively, the poem survives the death of the poet – and therefore the bodily home of the love it describes. But it can, miraculously, by its process of distillation, preserve an essence of that love which inspired it. This notion itself is a deeply romantic one. It's my hope that the reader will find a selection of poems here which – like Abelard and Héloïse – connect through words alone, and speak across the void between them of the most ordinary human marvel.

John Stammers, 2010

Love Poems

John Clare

First Love

I ne'er was struck before that hour
  With love so sudden and so sweet,
Her face it bloomed like a sweet flower
  And stole my heart away complete.
My face turned pale as deadly pale,
  My legs refused to walk away,
And when she looked, what could I ail?
  My life and all seemed turned to clay.

And then my blood rushed to my face
  And took my eyesight quite away,
The trees and bushes round the place
  Seemed midnight at noonday.
I could not see a single thing,
  Words from my eyes did start –
They spoke as chords do from the string,
  And blood burnt round my heart.

Are flowers the winter's choice?
  Is love's bed always snow?
She seemed to hear my silent voice,
  Not love's appeals to know.
I never saw so sweet a face
  As that I stood before.
My heart has left its dwelling-place
  And can return no more.

E. E. CUMMINGS

'since feeling is first'

since feeling is first
who pays any attention
to the syntax of things
will never wholly kiss you;

wholly to be a fool
while Spring is in the world

my blood approves,
and kisses are a far better fate
than wisdom
lady i swear by all flowers.   Don't cry
—the best gesture of my brain is less than
your eyelids' flutter which says

we are for each other: then
laugh, leaning back in my arms
for life's not a paragraph

And death i think is no parenthesis

A Birthday

My heart is like a singing bird
   Whose nest is in a watered shoot;
My heart is like an apple-tree
   Whose boughs are bent with thickset fruit;
My heart is like a rainbow shell
   That paddles in a halcyon sea;
My heart is gladder than all these
   Because my love is come to me.

Raise me a dais of silk and down;
   Hang it with vair and purple dyes;
Carve it in doves, and pomegranates,
   And peacocks with a hundred eyes;
Work it in gold and silver grapes,
   In leaves, and silver fleurs-de-lys;
Because the birthday of my life
   Is come, my love is come to me.

True Love

In the middle of the night, when we get up
after making love, we look at each other in
complete friendship, we know so fully
what the other has been doing. Bound to each other
like mountaineers coming down from a mountain,
bound with the tie of the delivery-room,
we wander down the hall to the bathroom, I can
hardly walk, I wobble through the granular
shadowless air, I know where you are
with my eyes closed, we are bound to each other
with huge invisible threads, our sexes
muted, exhausted, crushed, the whole
body a sex – surely this
is the most blessed time of my life,
our children asleep in their beds, each fate
like a vein of abiding mineral
not discovered yet. I sit
on the toilet in the night, you are somewhere in the room,
I open the window and snow has fallen in a
steep drift, against the pane, I
look up, into it,
a wall of cold crystals, silent
and glistening, I quietly call to you
and you come and hold my hand and I say
I cannot see beyond it. I cannot see beyond it.

Upon Julia's Clothes

Whenas in silks my Julia goes,
Till, then, methinks, how sweetly flows
That liquefaction of her clothes.

Next, when I cast mine eyes, and see
That brave vibration each way free,
O how that glittering taketh me !

JOHN BETJEMAN

A Subaltern's Love-Song

Miss J. Hunter Dunn, Miss J. Hunter Dunn,
Furnish'd and burnish'd by Aldershot sun,
What strenuous singles we played after tea,
We in the tournament – you against me!

Love-thirty, love-forty, oh! weakness of joy,
The speed of a swallow, the grace of a boy,
With carefullest carelessness, gaily you won,
I am weak from your loveliness, Joan Hunter Dunn.

Miss Joan Hunter Dunn, Miss Joan Hunter Dunn,
How mad I am, sad I am, glad that you won.
The warm-handled racket is back in its press,
But my shock-headed victor, she loves me no less.

Her father's euonymus shines as we walk,
And swing past the summer-house, buried in talk,
And cool the verandah that welcomes us in
To the six-o'clock news and a lime-juice and gin.

The scent of the conifers, sound of the bath,
The view from my bedroom of moss-dappled path,
As I struggle with double-end evening tie,
For we dance at the Golf Club, my victor and I.

On the floor of her bedroom lie blazer and shorts
And the cream-coloured walls are be-trophied with sports,
And westering, questioning settles the sun
On your low-leaded window, Miss Joan Hunter Dunn.

The Hillman is waiting, the light's in the hall,
The pictures of Egypt are bright on the wall,
My sweet, I am standing beside the oak stair
And there on the landing's the light on your hair.

By roads 'not adopted', by woodlanded ways,
She drove to the club in the late summer haze,
Into nine-o'clock Camberley, heavy with bells
And mushroomy, pine-woody, evergreen smells.

Miss Joan Hunter Dunn, Miss Joan Hunter Dunn,
I can hear from the car-park the dance has begun.
Oh! full Surrey twilight! importunate band!
Oh! strongly adorable tennis-girl's hand!

Around us are Rovers and Austins afar,
Above us, the intimate roof of the car,
And here on my right is the girl of my choice,
With the tilt of her nose and the chime of her voice,

And the scent of her wrap, and the words never said,
And the ominous, ominous dancing ahead.
We sat in the car-park till twenty to one
And now I'm engaged to Miss Joan Hunter Dunn.

ANDREW MARVELL

To His Coy Mistress

Had we but World enough, and Time
This coyness, Lady, were no crime,
We would sit down, and think which way
To walk, and pass our long Loves Day.
Thou by the Indian Ganges side
Should'st Rubies find: I by the Tide
Of Humber would complain. I would
Love you ten years before the Flood:
And you should, if you please, refuse
Till the Conversion of the Jews.
My vegetable Love should grow
Vaster than Empires, and more slow.
An hundred years should go to praise
Thine Eyes, and on thy Forehead gaze.
Two hundred to adore each Breast:
But thirty thousand to the rest.
An Age at least to every part,
And the last Age should show your Heart.
For, Lady, you deserve this State;
Nor would I love at lower rate.
　　But at my back I always hear
Times winged Charriot hurrying near:
And yonder all before us lye
Deserts of vast Eternity.
Thy Beauty shall no more be found;
Nor, in thy marble Vault, shall sound
My echoing Song: then Worms shall try
That long preserv'd Virginity:
And your quaint Honour turn to dust;

And into ashes all my Lust.
The Grave's a fine and private place,
But none, I think, do there embrace.
   Now therefore, while the youthful hew
Sits on thy skin like morning dew,
And while thy willing Soul transpires
At every pore with instant Fires,
Now let us sport us while we may;
And now, like am'rous birds of prey,
Rather at once our Time devour,
Than languish in his slow-chapt pow'r.
Let us roll all our Strength, and all
Our Sweetness, up into one Ball:
And tear our Pleasures with rough strife,
Thorough the Iron gates of Life.
Thus, though we cannot make our Sun
Stand still, yet we will make him run.

The Love Song of J. Alfred Prufrock

S'io credesse che mia risposta fosse
A persona che mai tornasse al mondo,
Questa fiamma staria senza più scosse.
Ma per ciò che giammai di questo fondo
Non tornò vivo alcun, s'i'odo il vero,
Senza tema d'infamia ti rispondo.

Let us go then, you and I,
When the evening is spread out against the sky
Like a patient etherised upon a table;
Let us go, through certain half-deserted streets,
The muttering retreats
Of restless nights in one-night cheap hotels
And sawdust restaurants with oyster-shells:
Streets that follow like a tedious argument
Of insidious intent
To lead you to an overwhelming question . . .
Oh, do not ask, "What is it?"
Let us go and make our visit.

In the room the women come and go
Talking of Michelangelo.

The yellow fog that rubs its back upon the window-panes,
The yellow smoke that rubs its muzzle on the window-panes
Licked its tongue into the corners of the evening.
Lingered upon the pools that stand in drains,
Let fall upon its back the soot that falls from chimneys,
Slipped by the terrace, made a sudden leap,
And seeing that it was a soft October night,
Curled once about the house, and fell asleep.

And indeed there will be time
For the yellow smoke that slides along the street,
Rubbing its back upon the window-panes;
There will be time, there will be time
To prepare a face to meet the faces that you meet;
There will be time to murder and create,
And time for all the works and days of hands
That lift and drop a question on your plate;
Time for you and time for me,
And time yet for a hundred indecisions,
And for a hundred visions and revisions,
Before the taking of a toast and tea.

In the room the women come and go
Talking of Michelangelo.

And indeed there will be time
To wonder, "Do I dare?" and, "Do I dare?"
Time to turn back and descend the stair,
With a bald spot in the middle of my hair—
(They will say: "How his hair is growing thin!")
My morning coat, my collar mounting firmly to the chin,
My necktie rich and modest, but asserted by a simple pin—
(They will say: "But how his arms and legs are thin!")
Do I dare
Disturb the universe?
In a minute there is time
For decisions and revisions which a minute will reverse.

For I have known them all already, known them all—
Have known the evenings, mornings, afternoons,
I have measured out my life with coffee spoons;
I know the voices dying with a dying fall
Beneath the music from a farther room.
　　So how should I presume?

And I have known the eyes already, known them all—
The eyes that fix you in a formulated phrase.
And when I am formulated, sprawling on a pin,
When I am pinned and wriggling on the wall,
Then how should I begin
To spit out all the butt-ends of my days and ways?
　　And how should I presume?

And I have known the arms already, known them all—
Arms that are braceleted and white and bare
(But in the lamplight, downed with light brown hair!)
Is it perfume from a dress
That makes me so digress?
Arms that lie along a table, or wrap about a shawl.
 And should I then presume?
 And how should I begin?

Shall I say, I have gone at dusk through narrow streets
And watched the smoke that rises from the pipes
Of lonely men in shirt-sleeves, leaning out of window? . . .

 I should have been a pair of ragged claws
Scuttling across the floors of silent seas.

And the afternoon, the evening, sleeps so peacefully!
Smoothed by long fingers,
Asleep . . . tired . . . or it malingers,
Stretched on the floor, here beside you and me.
Should I, after tea and cakes and ices,
Have the strength to force the moment to its crisis?
But though I have wept and fasted, wept and prayed,
Though I have seen my head (grown slightly bald) brought in
 upon a platter,
I am no prophet—and here's no great matter;
I have seen the moment of my greatness flicker,
And I have seen the eternal Footman hold my coat, and snicker,
And in short, I was afraid.

And would it have been worth it, after all,
After the cups, the marmalade, the tea,
Among the porcelain, among some talk of you and me,
Would it have been worth while,
To have bitten off the matter with a smile,
To have squeezed the universe into a ball
To roll it toward some overwhelming question,
To say: 'I am Lazarus, come from the dead,
Come back to tell you all, I shall tell you all'—
If one, settling a pillow by her head,
    Should say: 'That is not what I meant at all.
    That is not it, at all.'

And would it have been worth it, after all,
Would it have been worth while,
After the sunsets and the dooryards and the sprinkled streets,
After the novels, after the teacups, after the skirts that trail along
        the floor—
And this, and so much more?—
It is impossible to say just what I mean!
But as if a magic lantern threw the nerves in patterns on a screen:
Would it have been worth while
If one, settling a pillow or throwing off a shawl,
And turning toward the window, should say:
    'That is not it at all.
    That is not what I meant, at all.'

No! I am not Prince Hamlet, nor was meant to be;
Am an attendant lord, one that will do
To swell a progress, start a scene or two,
Advise the prince: no doubt, an easy tool,
Deferential, glad to be of use,
Politic, cautious, and meticulous;
Full of high sentence, but a bit obtuse;
At times, indeed, almost ridiculous—
Almost, at times, the Fool.

    I grow old . . . I grow old . . .
I shall wear the bottoms of my trousers rolled.

    Shall I part my hair behind? Do I dare to eat a peach?
I shall wear white flannel trousers, and walk upon the beach.
I have heard the mermaids singing, each to each.

    I do not think that they will sing to me.

    I have seen them riding seaward on the waves
Combing the white hair of the waves blown back
When the wind blows the water white and black.

    We have lingered in the chambers of the sea
By sea-girls wreathed with seaweed red and brown
Till human voices wake us, and we drown.

ALFRED, LORD TENNYSON

'If I were loved, as I desire to be'

If I were loved, as I desire to be,
What is there in this great sphere of earth,
And range of evil between death and birth,
That I should fear,—if I were loved by thee?
All the inner, all the outer world of pain
Clear love would pierce and cleave, if thou wert mine,
As I have heard that, somewhere in the main,
Fresh-water springs come up through bitter brine.
'Twere joy, not fear, clasped hand in hand with thee,
To wait for death—mute—careless of all ills,
Apart upon a mountain, though the surge
Of some new deluge from a thousand hills
Flung leagues of roaring foam into the gorge
Below us, as far on as eye could see.

Prayer To Be with Mercurial Women

Let me never have her father
call me, saying how's about
a round of golf? Instead I'll take
the grim, forbidding monster
who inspects me for a crooked
trouser crease. And spare me too
from palmy evenings which sail by
in restaurants, on barstools,
without a storming off or two.
'Darling, you were made for me.'
I pray I'll never hear those words.
I need to feel I'm stealing
love another man would kill for.
When in sleep she curls herself
around me, may she whisper names
that are not mine. I'd prefer
to be the second best she's had.
A curse on mouths which dovetail
as if there'd been a blueprint made:
I'd rather blush and slobber.
And once a month, please let me be
a punchbag. I'll take the blame
for everything: I want to taste
the stinging of a good slap.
I hope I'll find my begging notes
crumpled, torn in half, unread,
and when I phone, I want to hear
an endless sound of ringing.
Help me avoid the kind of girl

who means things when she says them,
unless she's screeching, telling me
exactly what I am. Amen.

'One day I wrote her name upon the strand'

One day I wrote her name upon the strand,
  But came the waves and washèd it away:
Again I wrote it with a second hand,
  But came the tide, and made my pains his prey.
'Vain man,' said she, 'thou do'st in vain assay,
  A mortal thing so to immortalize,
For I myself shall like to this decay,
  And eek my name be wipèd out likewise.'
'Not so,' quoth I, 'let baser things devise
  To die in dust, but you shall live by fame:
My verse your virtues rare shall eternize,
  And in the heavens write your glorious name,
    Where, whenas death shall all the world subdue,
    Our love shall live, and later life renew.'

House on the Beach

The shadows mediated by the slats of the venetian blind
stripe the silk finish ceiling;
I am reminded of the sheen of the ocean
of glossy magazine horoscopes I so deprecate,
am I not, after all, a logical and serious-minded Virgo?
Apparently, Venus is poorly aspected in Pisces
or something. I am all but nodding off at this point.

I expire across the bed with its sails full of disquietude,
its balsa-wood hull dipping and rising
on queasy unconsciousness like some Kon-Tiki
out to prove to me, as if I needed it,
that I am not new,
that I cannot get away from it all,
the it is all there is, and that my slumberings
retain the tell-tale signs of you
with your female body
and mouth full of explanations.
I fetch up onto this morning,
so strangely bright with exotic birds and fruit,
but still with its hoard of old stone heads.

But just how did it get here, this place –
in the margins of buying and selling
or from somewhere in the veneered wardrobe
between sharp suits, or materials
pre-weathered in the cutting room?
My new denim jacket has sand in its pockets,
that's how they distress them, you told me,

perhaps that's what the sand has done to me.
I am in distress, I had said (in body language
by rubbing the back of my neck) I am sand blasted!

Or did it float up among all the debris?
It could have bobbed in the cusp of beach and sea,
replete with the tactfully blanched flooring
and these hard little shells
that virtually stab your feet to death,
but that would be so hackneyed,
surely a place like this would be more original.

And another thing, who was it who said
don't build your house on sand?
Some old deity I think.
But rocks erode away into sand
and, like Thales said,
isn't everything just water anyway?
And he should know, having fallen down a well
trying to read the future in the stars.
And when everything is liquefied and clean,
wouldn't he be pleased, the old prognosticator,
if he himself hadn't already melted.

I strain to hear your breathing in almost the wash
of the water's edge and the lisping of the shingles
as they deliquesce into the sea;
I am asphyxiated with desire
to stroke the fine hairs of your body
and, as the sea runs over driftwood on the beach,
follow the subtle undulations of you.
I am filled up like an inflated tear
whose surface tension is so taut
that one more image of you with your poise –

your bare arms, your hands lightly crossed in front of you –
and I will break and shower into droplets like the waves
as they smash into the old wooden tide-breakers
and annihilate themselves in the air.

To Celia

Drink to me only with thine eyes,
   And I will pledge with mine;
Or leave a kiss within the cup,
   And I'll not look for wine.
The thirst that from the soul doth rise,
   Doth ask a drink divine;
But might I of Jove's nectar sup,
   I would not change for thine.

I sent thee late a rosy wreath,
   Not so much honouring thee,
As giving it a hope that there
   It could not withered be.
But thou thereon didst only breathe,
   And sent'st it back to me;
Since when it grows, and smells, I swear,
   Not of itself, but thee.

AUGUST KLEINZAHLER

Someone Named Gutierrez: a Dream, a Western

Outside the cantina
with you in the backseat of a ruined DeSoto,
torn upholstery, vinyl mange
and the big old radio's static frying
what could only be a Dixie Cups tune.
Things had gone terribly bad,
and Slim, who drove us the whole long way
through chaparral and dust,
was in there now, with them,
asking for the money he had no right to,
had no right to even ten years back
when the fire was, or so he says.
They nearly killed him then,
the fool, the braggart, the Suicide Kid,
just itching after a good old-timey
late afternoon cowboy send-off,
blood and gold and glinting sidearms,
with us stuck back there yet, hove-to
in the backseat like two kids
waiting for Dad.
                        When you touched me,
the lightest of touches, the most unforeseen,
carelessly along the wrist.
I nearly came unglued.
I mean, I knew about Ramon,
that lovely boy—and for so long,
the two of you. I cherish that photo still,
your white tam-o'-shanter, his red TransAm.
Then I became water.

Then, from what had once been my chest,
a plant made of light effloresced.
Thus, our adventure began, our slow-motion
free fall through the vapors and oils.
I stammered at your white flesh.
                              And that,
that's when the shooting began.

WILLIAM SHAKESPEARE

Sonnet 18

Shall I compare thee to a summer's day?
Thou art more lovely and more temperate.
Rough winds do shake the darling buds of May,
And summer's lease hath all too short a date:
Sometime too hot the eye of heaven shines,
And often is his gold complexion dimm'd;
And every fair from fair some time declines,
By chance, or nature's changing course, untrimm'd;
But thy eternal summer shall not fade
Nor lose possession of that fair thou ow'st;
Nor shall Death brag thou wand'rest in his shade,
When in eternal lines to time thou grow'st.
   So long as men can breathe or eyes can see,
   So long lives this, and this gives life to thee.

'Turn on your side and bear the day to me'

Turn on your side and bear the day to me
Beloved, sceptre-struck, immured
In the glass wall of sleep. Slowly
Uncloud the borealis of your eye
And show your iceberg secrets, your midnight prizes
To the green-eyed world and to me. Sin
Coils upward into thin air when you awaken
And again morning announces amnesty over
The serpent-kingdomed bed. Your mother
Watched with as dove an eye the unforgivable night
Sigh backward into innocence when you
Set a bright monument in her amorous sea.
Look down, Undine, on the trident that struck
Sons from the rock of vanity. Turn in the world
Sceptre-struck, spellbound, beloved,
Turn in the world and bear the day to me.

SIR WALTER SCOTT

An Hour with Thee

An hour with thee! When earliest day
  Dapples with gold the eastern gray,
Oh, what can frame my mind to bear
  The toil and turmoil, cark and care,
New griefs, which coming hours unfold,
And sad remembrance of the old?
  One hour with thee.

One hour with thee! When burning June
  Waves his red flag at pitch of noon;
What shall repay the faithful swain,
  His labour on the sultry plain;
And, more than cave or sheltering bough,
Cool feverish blood and throbbing brow?
  One hour with thee.

One hour with thee! When sun is set,
  Oh, what can teach me to forget
The thankless labours of the day;
  The hopes, the wishes, flung away;
The increasing wants, and lessening gains,
The master's pride, who scorns my pains?
  One hour with thee.

With Angels

(for Jonathon McCree)

It might start with a wing-tip, snuck
in your palm, hard beneath down, shy
as the nose of a well-mannered dog.
Don't push it. Don't shove yourself
under his ticklish wing, you don't
want to rest on that smooth
damask chest, feel his crucifix
twitch with each shocked boyish breath.

Wings are for flying. Imagine them:
flapping above you, freezing the sweat
on your hunched naked legs. They'd
tug him back with each thrust
like whiplash, like disgust, they'd
wrench up your hips to the crux of a *y*,
or suddenly out, a cork from a bottle.
And you can't fly, there's no getting round it.

If you clambered on top and squatted
with your thighs squashed like chicken,
or if you tried sideways, wings soft
on your flanks as a conference of moths,
you'd press the patterned feathers
out of weaving, of whack, you'd watch
the wings bent beneath you crack
on their arches, quills buckle like metal,

and pain crack his face like egg-glaze
on a fresco; and so wouldn't it end
with you going down as always,
him crossing his wings like a screen
on his chest? And as he shook and looked
to God, one hand vague on your nodding head,
would he weep, the way men do,
but pearls, or hard smalt angel tears?

John Anderson My Jo

John Anderson my jo, John,
   When we were first acquent;
Your locks were like the raven,
   Your bony brow was brent;
But now your brow is beld, John,
   Your locks are like the snaw;
But blessings on your frosty pow,
   John Anderson my Jo.

John Anderson my jo, John,
   We clamb the hill the gither;
And mony a canty day, John,
   We've had wi' ane anither:
Now we maun totter down, John,
   And hand in hand we'll go;
And sleep the gither at the foot,
   John Anderson my Jo.

Valentine

suck my red heart white, I will, because I love you, bless me,
o, and here, I will say, see I am back, in spite of you to bring
a gift I grew, it was busy in me once, filled the red branches
with blood, knocking like hope, beat time to my life's decline,
then followed after in its way, and did its duty.

JOHN DONNE

The Flea

Mark but this flea, and mark in this,
How little that which thou deny'st me is;
    Me it sucked first, and now sucks thee,
And in this flea, our two bloods mingled be;
    Confess it, this cannot be said
A sin, or shame, or loss of maidenhead,
    Yet this enjoys before it woo,
And pampered swells with one blood made of two,
And this, alas, is more than we would do.

Oh stay, three lives in one flea spare,
Where we almost, nay more than married are:
    This flea is you and I, and this
Our marriage bed, and marriage temple is;
    Though parents grudge, and you, we're met,
And cloistered in these living walls of jet.
    Though use make thee apt to kill me,
Let not to this, self murder added be,
And sacrilege, three sins in killing three.

Cruel and sudden, hast thou since
Purpled thy nail, in blood of innocence?
    In what could this flea guilty be,
Except in that drop which it sucked from thee?
    Yet thou triumph'st, and say'st that thou
Find'st not thyself, nor me the weaker now;
    'Tis true, then learn how false, fears be;
Just so much honour, when thou yield'st to me,
Will waste, as this flea's death took life from thee.

34

KATHLEEN JAMIE

The Swallows' Nest

(for P. B.)

Shutters, broken,
firewood, a rake, a wrought-
iron bed, the torch-lit
rafters of the lumber-room,
you showing me

one bird tucked in a home-
made bracket of spittle
and earth, while its mate slept
perched on the rim, at an angle
exact as a raised latch.

And You, Helen

And you, Helen, what should I give you?
So many things I would give you
Had I an infinite great store
Offered me and I stood before
To choose.   I would give you youth,
All kinds of loveliness and truth,
A clear eye as good as mine,
Lands, waters, flowers, wine,
As many children as your heart
Might wish for, a far better art
Than mine can be, all you have lost
Upon the travelling waters tossed,
Or given to me. If I could choose
Freely in that great treasure-house
Anything from any shelf,
I would give you back yourself,
And power to discriminate
What you want and want it not too late,
Many fair days free from care
And heart to enjoy both foul and fair,
And myself, too, if I could find
Where it lay hidden and it proved kind.

IAN DUHIG

From the Irish

According to Dineen, a Gael unsurpassed
in lexicographical enterprise, the Irish
for moon means 'the white circle in a slice
of half-boiled potato or turnip'. A star
is the mark on the forehead of a beast
and the sun is the bottom of a lake, or well.

Well, if I say to you your face
is like a slice of half-boiled turnip,
your hair is the colour of a lake's bottom
and at the centre of each of your eyes
is the mark of the beast, it is because
I want to love you properly, according to Dineen.

A Red Red Rose

O my Luve's like a red, red rose,
   That's newly sprung in June;
O my Luve's like the melodie
   That's sweetly play'd in tune. –

As fair art thou, my bonnie lass,
   So deep in luve am I;
And I will love thee still, my Dear,
   Till a' the seas gang dry. –

Till a' the seas gang dry, my Dear,
   And the rocks melt wi' the sun:
I will love thee still, my Dear,
   While the sands o' life shall run. –

And fare thee weel, my only Luve!
   And fare thee weel, a while!
And I will come again, my Luve,
   Tho' it were ten thousand mile!

CAROL ANN DUFFY

Valentine

Not a red rose or a satin heart.

I give you an onion.
It is a moon wrapped in brown paper.
It promises light
like the careful undressing of love.

Here.
It will blind you with tears
like a lover.
It will make your reflection
a wobbling photo of grief.

I am trying to be truthful.

Not a cute card or a kissogram.

I give you an onion.
Its fierce kiss will stay on your lips,
possessive and faithful
as we are,
for as long as we are.

Take it.
Its platinum loops shrink to a wedding-ring,
if you like.
Lethal.
Its scent will cling to your fingers,
cling to your knife.

from the Rubáiyát of Omar Khayyám

XI

HERE with a Loaf of Bread beneath the Bough,
A Flask of Wine, a Book of Verse—and Thou
    Beside me singing in the Wilderness—
And Wilderness is Paradise enow.

XII

"HOW sweet is mortal Sovranty!"—think some:
Others—"How blest the Paradise to come!"
    Ah, take the Cash in hand and wave the Rest;
Oh, the brave Music of a distant Drum!

XIII

LOOK to the Rose that blows about us "Lo,
"Laughing" she says, "into the World I blow;
    "At once the silken Tassel of my Purse
Tear, and its Treasure on the Garden throw."

XIV

THE Worldly Hope men set their Hearts upon
Turns Ashes—or it prospers; and anon,
    Like Snow upon the Desert's dusty Face
Lighting a little Hour or two—is gone.

Stargazing

The night is fine and dry. It falls and spreads
the cold sky with a million opposites
that, for a moment, seem like a million souls
and soon, none, and then, for what seems a long time,
one. Then of course it spins. What is better to do
than string out over the infinite dead spaces
the ancient beasts and spearmen of the human
mind, and, if not the real ones, new ones?

But, try making them clear to one you love –
whoever is standing by you is one you love
when pinioned by the stars – you will find it quite
impossible, but like her more for thinking
she sees that constellation.

After the wave of pain, you will turn to her
and, in an instant, change the universe
to a sky you were glad you came outside to see.

This is the act of all the descended gods
of every age and creed: to weary of all
that never ends, to take a human hand,
and go back into the house.

Arab Love-Song

THE hunchèd camels of the night
Trouble the bright
And silver waters of the moon.
The Maiden of the Morn will soon
Through Heaven stray and sing,
Star gathering.

Now while the dark about our loves is strewn,
Light of my dark, blood of my heart, O come!
And night will catch her breath up, and be dumb.

Leave thy father, leave thy mother
And thy brother;
Leave the black tents of thy tribe apart!
Am I not thy father and thy brother,
And thy mother?
And thou—what needest with thy tribe's black tents
Who hast the red pavilion of my heart?

Avenue A

We hardly ever see the moon any more
                              so no wonder
    it's so beautiful when we look up suddenly
and there it is gliding broken-faced over the bridges
brilliantly coursing, soft, and a cool wind fans
            your hair over your forehead and your memories
            of Red Grooms' locomotive landscape
I want some bourbon/you want some oranges/I love the leather
            jacket Norman gave me
                              and the corduroy coat David
    gave you, it is more mysterious than spring, the El Greco
heavens breaking open and then reassembling like lions
                              in a vast tragic veldt
    that is far from our small selves and our temporally united
passions in the cathedral of Januaries

    everything is too comprehensible
these are my delicate and caressing poems
I suppose there will be more of those others to come, as in the past
                              so many!
but for now the moon is revealing itself like a pearl
                    to my equally naked heart

Wild Nights—Wild Nights!

Wild Nights—Wild Nights!
Were I with thee
Wild Nights should be
Our luxury!

Futile—the Winds—
To a Heart in port—
Done with the Compass—
Done with the Chart!

Rowing in Eden—
Ah, the Sea!
Might I but moor—Tonight—
In Thee!

The Night We Stole a Full-Length Mirror

I'd have walked straight past if you hadn't said
Look at the moon and held my head in your hands
and turned it slowly round to face a skip,
its broken skyline of one-legged chair,
ripped out floor, till I saw it moving
– so slow, so bright – across the silver glass.
We stood there for ages, a bit drunk,
staring at the moon hanging there
as if it were for sale and we an old couple
weighing it up but knowing in our hearts
it is beyond us – A cat jumps out
and before we know it we're stealing back to my flat,
the great thing like a masterpiece in our hands,
its surface anxious with knees and knuckles,
the clenched line of your jaw and your lips
kissing the glass over and over with curses.
You lean it so it catches the bed and me,
I nudge it with my toe so it won't hold my head.
Switching off the light my skin turns blue
and when you come in on the scene and we see
ourselves like this we start to move like real
professionals and my head, disowned and free,
watches what our bodies are doing and somewhere
the thought *I can't believe we weren't made for this*
and I can't stop looking even though the ache
in my throat is growing and soon there will be tears
and I can hear you looking and I know what you're
looking at and it doesn't matter but it isn't me.
You left me behind in a bar in Copenhagen St,

the one with the small red lamps and my face hung
a hundred identical times along the stained wall
invoking like some old speaking doll
the dissatisfaction I come back and back to
and there's this really pretty Chinese waitress
you're trying not to look at while I'm talking to you.
Then you get up and I'm left alone so I lift my head to look
at the man who's been staring at me since I walked in.
He's huge and lonely and lifts his glass and nods
and all the women along the wall break into smiles.
Then you're back and whispering *your breasts your breasts*
and your hands are scrambling up the wet stone
of my back and I imagine the lonely man is there
behind the silver screen sipping his drink,
his eyes thick and moist behind the glass;
I know he's waiting to catch my eye but I won't
be seen to know I'm being watched. Not
till it's over and we collapse, all of a sudden
and awkward, and the room becomes itself again,
filling the mirror with its things, our two faces
staring in, calm and dull and self-absorbed.
Then we look at each other and are surprised
as if we weren't expecting to find the other
here and the smile is quick, like a nod slipped in
between two conspirators returned to the world
of daylight, birdsong, the good tug of guilt
before we tilt the mirror up-, sky-, heaven-ward.

JOHN DONNE

The Sun Rising

Busy old fool, unruly Sun,
　　Why dost thou thus,
Through windows and through curtains call on us?
Must to thy motions lovers' seasons run?
　　Saucy pedantic wretch, go chide
　　　Late school-boys, and sour 'prentices,
　　Go tell court-huntsmen that the King will ride,
　　Call country ants to harvest offices;
Love, all alike, no season knows, nor clime,
Nor hours, days, months, which are the rags of time.

　　Thy beams, so reverend and strong
　　　Why shouldst thou think?
I could eclipse and cloud them with a wink,
But that I would not lose her sight so long:
　　　If her eyes have not blinded thine,
　　　Look, and tomorrow late tell me,
　　Whether both the Indias of spice and mine
　　Be where thou left'st them, or lie here with me.
Ask for those kings whom thou saw'st yesterday,
And thou shalt hear, 'All here in one bed lay.'

She's all States, and all Princes I;
        Nothing else is.
Princes do but play us; compared to this,
All honour's mimic; all wealth alchemy.
        Thou, Sun, art half as happy as we,
        In that the world's contracted thus;
    Thine age asks ease, and since thy duties be
    To warm the world, that's done in warming us.
Shine here to us, and thou art everywhere;
This bed thy centre is, these walls thy sphere.

After Making Love We Hear Footsteps

For I can snore like a bullhorn
or play loud music
or sit up talking with any reasonably sober Irishman
and Fergus will only sink deeper
into his dreamless sleep, which goes by all in one flash,
but let there be that heavy breathing
or a stifled come-cry anywhere in the house
and he will wrench himself awake
and make for it on the run—as now, we lie together,
after making love, quiet, touching along the length of our bodies,
familiar touch of the long-married,
and he appears—in his baseball pajamas, it happens,
the neck opening so small he has to screw them on—
and flops down between us and hugs us and snuggles himself to sleep,
his face gleaming with satisfaction at being this very child.

In the half darkness we look at each other
and smile
and touch arms across this little, startlingly muscled body—
this one whom habit of memory propels to the ground of his making,
sleeper only the mortal sounds can sing awake,
this blessing love gives again into our arms.

Love's Philosophy

The fountains mingle with the river
   And the rivers with the Ocean,
The winds of Heaven mix for ever
   With a sweet emotion;
Nothing in the world is single;
   All things by a law divine
In one spirit meet and mingle.
   Why not I with thine? –

See the mountains kiss high Heaven
   And the waves clasp one another;
No sister-flower would be forgiven
   If it disdained its brother;
And the sunlight clasps the earth
   And the moonbeams kiss the sea:
What is all this sweet work worth
   If thou kiss not me?

Sometimes it happens

And sometimes it happens that you are friends and then
You are not friends,
And friendship has passed.
And whole days are lost and among them
A fountain empties itself.

And sometimes it happens that you are loved and then
You are not loved,
And love is past.
And whole days are lost and among them
A fountain empties itself into the grass.

And sometimes you want to speak to her and then
You do not want to speak,
Then the opportunity has passed.
Your dreams flare up, they suddenly vanish.

And also it happens that there is nowhere to go and then
There is somewhere to go,
Then you have bypassed.
And the years flare up and are gone,
Quicker than a minute.

So you have nothing.
You wonder if these things matter and then
As soon as you begin to wonder if these things matter
They cease to matter,
And caring is past.
And a fountain empties itself into the grass.

'Love? Do I love? I walk'

Love?   Do I love?   I walk
Within the brilliance of another's thought,
As in a glory.   I was dark before,
As Venus' chapel in the black of night:
But there was something holy in the darkness,
Softer and not so thick as other where;
And, as rich moonlight may be to the blind,
Unconsciously consoling.   Then love came,
Like the out-bursting of a trodden star,
And what before was hueless and unseen
Now shows me a divinity, like that
Which, raised to life out of the snowy rock,
Surpass'd mankind's creation, and repaid
Heaven for Pandora.

CAROL ANN DUFFY

Rapture

Thought of by you all day, I think of you.
The birds sing in the shelter of a tree.
Above the prayer of rain, unacred blue,
not paradise, goes nowhere endlessly.
How does it happen that our lives can drift
far from our selves, while we stay trapped in time,
queuing for death? It seems nothing will shift
the pattern of our days, alter the rhyme
we make with loss to assonance with bliss.
Then love comes, like a sudden flight of birds
from earth to heaven after rain. Your kiss,
recalled, unstrings, like pearls, this chain of words.
Huge skies connect us, joining here to there.
Desire and passion on the thinking air.

W. B. YEATS

Down by the Salley Gardens

Down by the salley gardens my love and I did meet;
She passed the salley gardens with little snow-white feet.
She bid me take love easy, as the leaves grow on the tree;
But I, being young and foolish, with her would not agree.

In a field by the river my love and I did stand,
And on my leaning shoulder she laid her snow-white hand.
She bid me take life easy, as the grass grows on the weirs;
But I was young and foolish, and now am full of tears.

JOHN BETJEMAN

In a Bath Teashop

'Let us not speak, for the love we bear one another—
  Let us hold hands and look.'
She, such a very ordinary little woman;
  He, such a thumping crook:
But both, for the moment, little lower than the angels
  In the teashop inglenook.

'This living hand, now warm and capable'

This living hand, now warm and capable
Of earnest grasping, would, if it were cold
And in the icy silence of the tomb,
So haunt thy days and chill thy dreaming nights
That thou wouldst wish thine own heart dry of blood
So in my veins red life might stream again,
And thou be conscience-calmed – see here it is –
I hold it towards you.

MICHAEL DONAGHY

The Present

For the present there is just one moon,
though every level pond gives back another.

But the bright disc shining in the black lagoon,
perceived by astrophysicist and lover,

is milliseconds old. And even that light's
seven minutes older than its source.

And the stars we think we see on moonless nights
are long extinguished. And, of course,

this very moment, as you read this line,
is literally gone before you know it.

Forget the here-and-now. We have no time
but this device of wantonness and wit.

Make me this present then: your hand in mine,
and we'll live out our lives in it.

'Bright star! Would I were steadfast as thou art'

Bright star! would I were steadfast as thou art—
   Not in lone splendour hung aloft the night
And watching, with eternal lids apart,
   Like nature's patient, sleepless Eremite,
The moving waters at their priestlike task
   Of pure ablution round earth's human shores,
Or gazing on the new soft fallen mask
   Of snow upon the mountains and the moors—
   No—yet still steadfast, still unchangeable,
Pillowed upon my fair love's ripening breast,
To feel for ever its soft fall and swell,
   Awake for ever in a sweet unrest,
Still, still to hear her tender-taken breath,
And so live ever—or else swoon to death.

W. H. AUDEN

Lullaby

Lay your sleeping head, my love,
Human on my faithless arm;
Time and fevers burn away
Individual beauty from
Thoughtful children, and the grave
Proves the child ephemeral:
But in my arms till break of day
Let the living creature lie,
Mortal, guilty, but to me
The entirely beautiful.

Soul and body have no bounds:
To lovers as they lie upon
Her tolerant enchanted slope
In their ordinary swoon,
Grave the vision Venus sends
Of supernatural sympathy,
Universal love and hope;
While an abstract insight wakes
Among the glaciers and the rocks
The hermit's sensual ecstasy.

Certainty, fidelity
On the stroke of midnight pass
Like vibrations of a bell,
And fashionable madmen raise
Their pedantic boring cry:
Every farthing of the cost,
All the dreaded cards foretell,
Shall be paid, but from this night
Not a whisper, not a thought,
Not a kiss nor look be lost.

Beauty, midnight, vision dies:
Let the winds of dawn that blow
Softly round your dreaming head
Such a day of sweetness show
Eye and knocking heart may bless,
Find the mortal world enough;
Noons of dryness see you fed
By the involuntary powers,
Nights of insult let you pass
Watched by every human love.

Song

Ae fond kiss, and then we sever;
Ae fareweel, and then for ever!
Deep in heart-wrung tears I'll pledge thee,
Warring sighs and groans I'll wage thee. –

Who shall say that Fortune grieves him,
While the star of hope she leaves him:
Me, nae chearful twinkle lights me;
Dark despair around benights me. –

I'll ne'er blame my partial fancy,
Naething could resist my Nancy:
But to see her, was to love her;
Love but her, and love for ever. –

Had we never lov'd sae kindly,
Had we never lov'd sae blindly!
Never met – or never parted,
We had ne'er been broken-hearted. –

Fare-thee-weel, thou first and fairest!
Fare-thee-weel, thou best and dearest!
Thine be ilka joy and treasure,
Peace, Enjoyment, Love and Pleasure! –

Ae fond kiss, and then we sever!
Ae fareweel, Alas, for ever!
Deep in heart-wrung tears I'll pledge thee,
Warring sighs and groans I'll wage thee. –

The Kiss

My mouth blooms like a cut.
I've been wronged all year, tedious
nights, nothing but rough elbows in them
and delicate boxes of Kleenex calling *crybaby*
crybaby, you fool!

Before today my body was useless.
Now it's tearing at its square corners.
It's tearing old Mary's garments off, knot by knot
and see — Now it's shot full of these electric bolts.
Zing! A resurrection!

Once it was a boat, quite wooden
and with no business, no salt water under it
and in need of some paint. It was no more
than a group of boards. But you hoisted her, rigged her.
She's been elected.

My nerves are turned on. I hear them like
musical instruments. Where there was silence
the drums, the strings are incurably playing. You did this.
Pure genius at work. Darling, the composer has stepped
into fire.

JOHN DONNE

A Valediction: Forbidding Mourning

As virtuous men pass mildly away,
  And whisper to their souls, to go,
Whilst some of their sad friends do say,
  The breath goes now, and some say, no:

So let us melt, and make no noise,
  No tear-floods, nor sigh-tempests move,
'Twere profanation of our joys
  To tell the laity our love.

Moving of th' earth brings harms and fears,
  Men reckon what it did and meant,
But trepidation of the spheres,
  Though greater far, is innocent.

Dull sublunary lovers' love
  (Whose soul is sense) cannot admit
Absence, because it doth remove
  Those things which elemented it.

But we by a love, so much refined,
  That our selves know not what it is,
Inter-assured of the mind,
  Care less, eyes, lips, and hands to miss.

Our two souls therefore, which are one,
Though I must go, endure not yet
A breach, but an expansion,
Like gold to aery thinness beat.

If they be two, they are two so
   As stiff twin compasses are two,
Thy soul the fixed foot, makes no show
   To move, but doth, if th'other do.

And though it in the centre sit,
   Yet when the other far doth roam,
It leans, and hearkens after it,
   And grows erect, as that comes home.

Such wilt thou be to me, who must
   Like th' other foot, obliquely run;
Thy firmness makes my circle just,
   And makes me end, where I begun.

FRANK O'HARA

To the Harbormaster

I wanted to be sure to reach you;
though my ship was on the way it got caught
in some moorings. I am always tying up
and then deciding to depart. In storms and
at sunset, with the metallic coils of the tide
around my fathomless arms, I am unable
to understand the forms of my vanity
or I am hard alee with my Polish rudder
in my hand and the sun sinking. To
you I offer my hull and the tattered cordage
of my will. The terrible channels where
the wind drives me against the brown lips
of the reeds are not all behind me. Yet
I trust the sanity of my vessel; and
if it sinks, it may well be in answer
to the reasoning of the eternal voices,
the waves which have kept me from reaching you.

'When we two parted'

When we two parted
In silence and tears,
Half broken-hearted,
To sever for years,
Pale grew thy cheek and cold,
Colder thy kiss;
Truly that hour foretold
Sorrow to this.

The dew of the morning
Sank chill on my brow
It felt like the warning
Of what I feel now.
Thy vows are all broken,
And light is thy fame:
I hear thy name spoken,
And share in its shame.

They name thee before me,
A knell to mine ear;
A shudder comes o'er me
Why wert thou so dear?
They know not I knew thee,
Who knew thee too well:
Long, long shall I rue thee
Too deeply to tell.

In secret we met
In silence I grieve
That thy heart could forget,
Thy spirit deceive.
If I should meet thee
After long years,
How should I greet thee?
With silence and tears.

Prayer

God give me strength to lead a double life.
Cut me in half.
Make each half happy in its own way
with what is left. Let me disobey
my own best instincts
and do what I want to do, whatever that may be,
without regretting it, or thinking I might.

When I come home late at night from home,
saying I have to go away,
remind me to look out the window
to see which house I'm in.
Pin a smile on my face
when I turn up two weeks later with a tan
and presents for everyone.

Teach me how to stand and where to look
when I say the words
about where I've been
and what sort of time I've had.
Was it good or bad or somewhere in between?
I'd like to know how I feel about these things,
perhaps you'd let me know?

When it's time to go to bed in one of my lives,
go ahead of me up the stairs,
shine a light in the corners of my room.
Tell me this: do I wear pyjamas here,
or sleep with nothing on?
If you can't oblige by cutting me in half,
God give me strength to lead a double life.

WILLIAM BLAKE

The Sick Rose

O rose, thou art sick!
The invisible worm
That flies in the night,
In the howling storm,

Has found out thy bed
Of crimson joy,
And his dark secret love
Does thy life destroy.

Adultery

Wear dark glasses in the rain.
Regard what was unhurt
as though through a bruise.
Guilt. A sick, green tint.

New gloves, money tucked in the palms,
the handshake crackles. Hands
can do many things. Phone.
Open the wine. Wash themselves. Now

you are naked under your clothes all day,
slim with deceit. Only the once
brings you alone to your knees,
miming, more, more, older and sadder,

creative. Suck a lie with a hole in it
on the way home from a lethal, thrilling night
up against a wall, faster. Language
unpeels to a lost cry. You're a bastard.

Do it do it do it. Sweet darkness
in the afternoon; a voice in your ear
telling you how you are wanted,
which way, now. A telltale clock

wiping the hours from its face, your face
on a white sheet, gasping, radiant, yes.
Pay for it in cash, fiction, cab-fares back
to the life which crumbles like a wedding-cake.

Paranoia for lunch; too much
to drink, as a hand on your thigh
tilts the restaurant. You know all about love,
don't you. Turn on your beautiful eyes

for a stranger who's dynamite in bed, again
and again; a slow replay in the kitchen
where the slicing of innocent onions
scalds you to tears. Then, selfish autobiographical sleep

in a marital bed, the tarnished spoon of your body
stirring betrayal, your heart over-ripe at the core.
You're an expert, darling; your flowers
dumb and explicit on nobody's birthday.

So write the script – illness and debt,
a ring thrown away in a garden
no moon can heal, your own words
commuting to bile in your mouth, terror –

and all for the same thing twice. And all
for the same thing twice. You did it.
What. Didn't you. Fuck. Fuck. No. That was
the wrong verb. This is only an abstract noun.

JOHN DRYDEN

Farewell Ungrateful Traitor

Farewell ungrateful traitor,
　　Farewell my perjured swain,
Let never injured creature
　　Believe a man again.
The pleasure of possessing
Surpasses all expressing,
But 'tis too short a blessing,
　　And love too long a pain.

'Tis easy to deceive us
　　In pity of your pain,
But when we love you leave us
　　To rail at you in vain.
Before we have descried it,
There is no bliss beside it,
But she that once has tried it
　　Will never love again.

The passion you pretended
　　Was only to obtain,
But when the charm is ended
　　The charmer you disdain.
Your love by ours we measure
Till we have lost our treasure,
But dying is a pleasure,
　　When living is a pain.

A Private Bottling

So I will go, then. I would rather grieve over your
absence than over you.

— Antonio Porchia

Back in the same room that an hour ago
we had led, lamp by lamp, into the darkness
I sit down and turn the radio on low
as the last girl on the planet still awake
reads a dedication to the ships
and puts on a recording of the ocean.

I carefully arrange a chain of nips
in a big fairy-ring; in each square glass
the tincture of a failed geography,
its dwindled burns and woodlands, whin-fires, heather,
the sklent of its wind and its salty rain,
the love-worn habits of its working-folk,
the waveform of their speech, and by extension
how they sing, make love, or take a joke.

So I have a good nose for this sort of thing.

Then I will suffer kiss after fierce kiss
letting their gold tongues slide along my tongue
as each gives up, in turn, its little song
of the patient years in glass and sherry-oak,
the shy negotiations with the sea,
air and earth, the trick of how the peat-smoke
was shut inside it, like a black thought.

Tonight I toast her with the extinct malts
of Ardlussa, Ladyburn and Dalintober
and an ancient pledge of passionate indifference:
Ochon o do dhóigh mé mo chlairsach ar a shon,
wishing her health, as I might wish her weather.

When the circle is closed and I have drunk myself sober
I will tilt the blinds a few degrees, and watch
the dawn grow in a glass of liver-salts,
wait for the birds, the milk-float's sweet nothings,
then slip back to the bed where she lies curled,
replace the live egg of her burning ass
gently, in the cold nest of my lap,
as dead to her as she is to the world.

*

Here we are again; it is precisely
twelve, fifteen, thirty years down the road
and one turn higher up the spiral chamber
that separates the burnt ale and dark grains
of what I know, from what I can remember.
Now each glass holds its micro-episode
in permanent suspension, like a movie-frame
on acetate, until it plays again,
revivified by a suave connoisseurship
that deepens in the silence and the dark
to something like an infinite sensitivity.
This is no romantic fantasy: my father
used to know a man who'd taste the sea,
then leave his nets strung out along the bay
because there were no fish in it that day.
Everything is in everything else. It is a matter
of attunement, as once, through the hiss and backwash,
I steered the dial into the voice of God

slightly to the left of Hilversum,
half-drowned by some big, blurry waltz
the way some stars obscure their dwarf companions
for centuries, till someone thinks to look.

In the same way, I can isolate the feints
of feminine effluvia, carrion, shite,
those rogues and toxins only introduced
to give the composition a little weight
as rough harmonics do the violin-note
or Pluto, Cheiron and the lesser saints
might do to our lives, for all you know.
(By Christ, you would recognise their absence
as anyone would testify, having sunk
a glass of *North British*, run off a patent still
in some sleet-hammered satellite of Edinburgh:
a bleak spirit, no amount of caramel
could sweeten or disguise, its after-effect
somewhere between a blanket-bath and a sad wank.
There is, no doubt, a bar in Lothian
where it is sworn upon and swallowed neat
by furloughed riggers and the Special Police,
men who hate the company of women.)

O whiskies of Long Island and Provence!
This little number catches at the throat
but is all sweetness in the finish: my tongue trips
first through burning brake-fluid, then nicotine,
pastis, *Diorissimo* and wet grass;
another is silk sleeves and lip-service
with a kick like a smacked face in a train-station;
another, the light charge and the trace of zinc
tap-water picks up at the moon's eclipse.
You will know the time I mean by this.

Because your singular absence, in your absence,
has bred hard, tonight I take the waters
with the whole clan: our faceless ushers, bridesmaids,
our four Shelties, three now ghosts of ghosts;
our douce sons and our lovely loudmouthed daughters
who will, by this late hour, be fully grown,
perhaps with unborn children of their own.
So finally, let me propose a toast:
not to love, or life, or real feeling,
but to their sentimental residue;
to your sweet memory, but not to you.

The sun will close its circle in the sky
before I close my own, and drain the purely
offertory glass that tastes of nothing
but silence, burnt dust on the valves, and whisky.

'So, we'll go no more a-roving'

So, we'll go no more a-roving
  So late into the night,
Though the heart be still as loving,
  And the moon be still as bright.

For the sword outwears its sheath,
  And the soul wears out the breast,
And the heart must pause to breathe,
  And love itself have rest.

Though the night was made for loving,
  And the day returns too soon,
Yet we'll go no more a-roving
  By the light of the moon.

Tarantella

Do you remember an Inn,
Miranda?
Do you remember an Inn?
And the tedding and the spreading
Of the straw for a bedding,
And the fleas that tease in the High Pyrenees,
And the wine that tasted of the tar?
And the cheers and the jeers of the young muleteers
(Under the vine of the dark verandah)?
Do you remember an Inn, Miranda,
Do you remember an Inn?
And the cheers and the jeers of the young muleteers
Who hadn't got a penny,
And who weren't paying any,
And the hammer at the doors and the Din?
And the Hip! Hop! Hap!
Of the clap
Of the hands to the twirl and the swirl
Of the girl gone chancing,
Glancing,
Dancing,
Backing and advancing,
Snapping of a clapper to the spin
Out and in –
And the Ting, Tong, Tang of the Guitar!
Do you remember an Inn,
Miranda?
Do you remember an Inn!

Never more;
Miranda,
Never more.
Only the high peaks hoar:
And Aragon a torrent at the door.
No sound
In the walls of the Halls where falls
The tread
Of the feet of the dead to the ground
No sound:
But the boom
Of the far Waterfall like Doom.

À Quoi Bon Dire

Seventeen years ago you said
Something that sounded like Good-bye;
    And everybody thinks that you are dead,
        But I.

So I, as I grow stiff and cold
To this and that say Good-bye too;
    And everybody sees that I am old
        But you.

And one fine morning in a sunny lane
Some boy and girl will meet and kiss and swear
    That nobody can love their way again
        While over there
You will have smiled, I shall have tossed your hair.

E. E. CUMMINGS

'somewhere i have never travelled,gladly beyond'

somewhere i have never travelled,gladly beyond
any experience,your eyes have their silence:
in your most frail gesture are things which enclose me,
or which i cannot touch because they are too near

your slightest look easily will unclose me
though i have closed myself as fingers,
you open always petal by petal myself as Spring opens
(touching skilfully,mysteriously)her first rose

or if your wish be to close me,i and
my life will shut very beautifully,suddenly,
as when the heart of this flower imagines
the snow carefully everywhere descending;

nothing which we are to perceive in this world equals
the power of your intense fragility:whose texture
compels me with the colour of its countries,
rendering death and forever with each breathing

(i do not know what it is about you that closes
and opens;only something in me understands
the voice of your eyes is deeper than all roses)
nobody,not even the rain,has such small hands

ELIZABETH BARRETT BROWNING

Sonnets From the Portuguese (xliii)

How do I love thee? Let me count the ways.
I love thee to the depth and breadth and height
My soul can reach, when feeling out of sight
For the ends of Being and ideal Grace.
I love thee to the level of every day's
Most quiet need, by sun and candlelight.
I love thee freely, as men strive for Right;
I love thee purely, as they turn from Praise.
I love thee with the passion put to use
In my old griefs, and with my childhood's faith.
I love thee with a love I seemed to lose
With my lost saints, – I love thee with the breath,
Smiles, tears, of all my life! – and, if God choose,
I shall but love thee better after death.

Love

So, the year's done with!
  (Love me for ever!)
All March begun with,
  April's endeavour;
May-wreaths that bound me
  June needs must sever;
Now snows fall round me,
Quenching June's fever –
  (Love me for ever!)

CHRISTOPHER MARLOWE

The Passionate Shepherd to His Love

Come live with me, and be my love,
And we will all the pleasures prove,
That valleys, groves, hills and fields,
Woods, or steepy mountain yields.

And we will sit upon the rocks,
Seeing the shepherds feed their flocks
By shallow rivers, to whose falls
Melodious birds sing madrigals.

And I will make thee beds of roses,
And a thousand fragrant posies,
A cap of flowers and a kirtle
Embroidered all with leaves of myrtle.

A gown made of the finest wool
Which from our pretty lambs we pull,
Fair lined slippers for the cold,
With buckles of the purest gold;

A belt of straw and ivy-buds,
With coral clasps and amber studs,
And if these pleasures may thee move,
Come live with me, and be my love.

The shepherd swains shall dance and sing
For thy delight each May-morning,
If these delights thy mind may move;
Then live with me, and be my love.

Like What You Get When You Play It Backwards

I knew a man who had a way with women.
He'd come in and sit down at a table and talk
them into bed. And when you considered the others,
the regulars - with their constructs about life,
their Gauloises, their lingo, their Zippo lighters,
their aviator jackets with *The Glass Bead Game* protruding –
it made a lot of sense. He hardly ever had any
cigarettes. And always said 'May I have a cigarette?'
Then he would describe a prototype machine of his
for listening to music while walking down the street
or he'd make a drawing on the inner lip of a fag packet
of the scapula of a long-extinct amphibian horse
or the configuration of classical London squares,
or a most wonderful fish soup someone called Monique
had made for him. But he never gave away too much –
no sectioning orders, no feuds with estranged wives,
and nothing that would set you on a pedestal.
Sometimes he'd open a piece of paper on which
there were long lists of words: I remember 'sackbut',
and also 'vestibule'. This was before films began
to be made about people like him so you weren't thinking
"Hey, where've I heard that before?" Yes, there was
something Buster Keatonesque in the clarity of his iris
and in his nude appeal. Once I saw a girl playing
with the red wax pooling down from the candle
in the bottle that others had been playing with
and he took her hands in his and said *Don't* and she stopped.

PERCY BYSSHE SHELLEY

One Word Is Too Often Profaned

One word is too often profaned
    For me to profane it,
One feeling too falsely disdained
    For thee to disdain it;
One hope is too like despair
    For prudence to smother,
And pity from thee more dear
    Than that from another.

I can give not what men call love;
    But wilt thou accept not
The worship the heart lifts above
    And the Heavens reject not,–
The desire of the moth for the star,
    Of the night for the morrow,
The devotion to something afar
    From the sphere of our sorrow?

from 'Songs for Swingeing Lovers'

Living in Sin

Hide the pink toothbrush, the dark nest of knickers,
the loofah, the fake fur, the eau de toilette;
sling all that yoghurt and climb in this cupboard:
they're trying to cut off our benefit.

Bacon and Eggs

Breakfast. In a fat-splashed gown
   your working model fitted:
'The chicken is only involved
   but the pig, the pig is committed.'

Sonnet 116

Let me not to the marriage of true minds
Admit impediments. Love is not love
Which alters when it alteration finds,
Or bends with the remover to remove.
O, no! it is an ever-fixed mark,
That looks on tempests, and is never shaken;
It is the star to every wand'ring bark,
Whose worth's unknown, although his height be taken.
Love's not Time's fool, though rosy lips and cheeks
Within his bending sickle's compass come;
Love alters not with his brief hours and weeks,
But bears it out even to the edge of doom.
   If this be error, and upon me prov'd,
    I never writ, nor no man ever lov'd.

Nevers

Passions never spoken,
never broken but preserved,
never layered under marriages
or burnt to dust by fast affairs
are saints to us,

the sacred ones,
bodily enshrined
to lie in state like Bernadette
at Nevers of the mind;
amazing, garlanded and fair.

Older, at the inkling
of an accent or a smile,
we travel there.

The Farmer's Bride

To ——
He asked life of thee, and thou gavest him a long life:
even for ever and ever.

Three Summers since I chose a maid,
Too young maybe—but more's to do
At harvest-time than bide and woo.
    When us was wed she turned afraid
Of love and me and all things human;
Like the shut of a winter's day.
Her smile went out, and 'twasn't a woman–
    More like a little frightened fay.
        One night, in the Fall, she runned away.

"Out 'mong the sheep, her be," they said,
'Should properly have been abed;
But sure enough she wasn't there
Lying awake with her wide brown stare.
So over seven-acre field and up-along across the down
    We chased her, flying like a hare
Before our lanterns. To Church-Town
    All in a shiver and a scare
We caught her, fetched her home at last
And turned the key upon her, fast.

She does the work about the house
As well as most, but like a mouse:
    Happy enough to chat and play
    With birds and rabbits and such as they,
    So long as men-folk keep away.
"Not near, not near!" her eyes beseech
When one of us comes within reach.
    The women say that beasts in stall
    Look round like children at her call.
    I've hardly heard her speak at all.

Shy as a leveret, swift as he,
Straight and slight as a young larch tree,
Sweet as the first wild violets, she,
To her wild self. But what to me?

The short days shorten and the oaks are brown,
    The blue smoke rises to the low grey sky,
One leaf in the still air falls slowly down,
    A magpie's spotted feathers lie
On the black earth spread white with rime,
The berries redden up to Christmas-time.
    What's Christmas-time without there be
    Some other in the house than we!

    She sleeps up in the attic there
    Alone, poor maid. 'Tis but a stair
Betwixt us. Oh! my God! the down,
The soft young down of her, the brown,
The brown of her—her eyes, her hair, her hair!

The Soldier's Girl

I've never held a gun, but knew
if I did it would be like this:
in a red nightdress in a foreign town,
a smell of chicken clinging
in the curtains, a man standing over me
saying *Never touch it,*
                            then taking me through it.
Stiff with gold buttons and starch, you slide
the magazine in, draw the barrel, cock,
slick as a dealer's shuffle, part brag,
part second nature, hand it to me, packed
like a dead man's head. I raise, pull
the trigger. It's slight as a key turning,
the high click carrying the relief
of every Russian roulette scene. But I let
the safety-catch lecture, mechanical
breakdown, count of sixteen bullets (strapped
ready for action) wash over.
                            I'm afraid
of fluency. Take standing in a bar,
a stranger's mouth dry and silent,
so close you see pupils crawl open
like ink on cartridge paper, the tremors
of each hair, feel the pull of heat inches
from you.
            This childish giving in to instinct
could squeeze fingers round a gun, engulfing
as a blush. And take that scene: me worse for wear,
unable to see a line, let alone draw it.

You in the doorway; the hot recognition
of my white arms sprawled across another
man's neck kick-starting fury, easy
as a light switch, and jarring your eyes'
membrane for seconds before black.

ANNE BRADSTREET

To My Dear and Loving Husband

If ever two were one, then surely we.
If ever man were lov'd by wife, then thee;
If ever wife was happy in a man,
Compare with me ye women if you can.
I prize thy love more than whole Mines of gold,
Or all the riches that the East doth hold.
My love is such that Rivers cannot quench,
Nor ought but love from thee, give recompense.
Thy love is such I can no way repay,
The heavens reward thee manifold, I pray.
Then while we live, in love let's so persevere,
That when we live no more, we may live ever.

The Best Man That Ever Was

I was never expected to sign the register
    as all was pre-arranged by his general staff,
but I did it out of choice and for the image that I made
    with the stewards and the bellboys,
my gloves laid side by side, and his Party rings that I hid
    from my family (it was torment, the life
in my family home, everyone smoking and rows
    about guns and butter at every inedible meal
and my aunts in their unhinged state, threatening suicide),
    and as I wrote my signature along the line
the letters seemed to coil like the snake
    saying, *I am here to be with Him.*

There were always little jobs to do
    in preparation for his coming – dinner to order,
consideration of the wine-list, hanging up my robe,
    a dab of perfume on my palms.
But it was never long before I found the need to pay
    attention to the corded sheaf of birch twigs
brought from home to service our love-making.
    How he loved to find it, ready for his use,
homely on a sheet of common newspaper –
    A Thing of Nature, so he said, *so fine, so pure.*
He'd turn away and smooth his thinning hair,
    lost as he was in some vision of grandeur.

And having washed and dried his hands with care
    and filled our flutes like any ordinary man,
the night's first task would come into his mind.
    He'd bark his hoarse, articulate command
and down I'd bend across the ornamented desk,
    my mouth level with the inkstand's claws,
my cheek flat against the blotter; I'd lift my skirts,
    slip down my panties and sob for him
with every blow. And I saw visions of my own: daisies,
    sometimes brown contented cows, dancers' puffy skirts,
a small boat adrift on a choppy sea; and once a lobster sang
    to me: *Happy Days Are Here Again!*

He'd tut at the marks and help me to my feet
    and we'd proceed into the dining room
and laugh and drink and raise the silver domes
    on turbot, plover and bowls of zabaglione.
You'd think he'd never seen a woman eat. Once he took
    my spoon out of my hand and asked me, *Are you happy?*
I'd serve him coffee by the fire and tend the logs.
    He'd unknot his tie. I'd comb my hair.
He'd make a phone call to no one of importance
    and we'd prepare for rest. There never was a man
so ardent in the invocation of love's terms:
    liebling, liebchen, mein liebe, mein kleine liebe!

and always the same – and in the acts: the frog, the hound,
    the duck, the goddess, the bear, the boar,
the whale, the galleon and the important artist –
    always in the order he preferred –
eyes shut and deaf to the world's abhorrence
    churning and churning in his stinking heaven.
It's over. But it is still good to arrive at a fine hotel
    and reward the major-domo's gruff punctilio
with a smile and a tip and let the bellboys slap my arse
    and remember him, the man who thrashed me,
fed me, adored me. He was the best man that ever was.
    He was my assassin of the world.

Methought I Saw My Late Espousèd Saint

Methought I saw my late espousèd Saint
　　Brought to me like Alcestis from the grave,
　　Whom Jove's great Son to her glad Husband gave,
　　Rescu'd from death by force though pale and faint.
Mine as whom washt from spot of child-bed taint,
　　Purification in the old Law did save,
　　And such, as yet once more I trust to have
　　Full sight of her in Heaven without restraint,
Came vested all in white, pure as her mind:
　　Her face was vail'd, yet to my fancied sight,
　　Love, sweetness, goodness, in her person shin'd
So clear, as in no face with more delight.
　　But O as to embrace me she enclin'd
　　I wak'd, she fled, and day brought back my night.

AꓭBA CD

O verily you were readily forgot
until, spring-cleaning, I happened upon my 'best of' Abba CD,
became engulfed in the golden chords of *Knowing Me,*
Knowing You, as those resourceful Swedes, so apt and ageless at regret

played on, song after song, and suddenly your body-heat
was burned back into me. O Benny and Bjorn, hamster-faced Svengali's,
how your verse/chorus - middle-eight - verse/chorus excoriates me,
excoriates the delicate

membrane of avoidance, for when Agnetha, embodiment of
                    exultant melancho
-lia, stands back to back with the other one -the redhead-
[un]heroically rhyming 'Glasgow' with 'last show'

it raises your spectre back from the dead
trilling a supe-per-per, troup-per-per of Scandinavian brio
until you retreat down a secret track, in a white shift, etiolated.

WILLIAM SHAKESPEARE

Sonnet 130

My mistress' eyes are nothing like the sun;
Coral is far more red than her lips' red;
If snow be white, why then her breasts are dun;
If hairs be wires, black wires grow on her head.
I have seen roses damask'd, red and white,
But no such roses see I in her cheeks;
And in some perfumes is there more delight
Than in the breath that from my mistress reeks.
I love to hear her speak, yet well I know
That music hath a far more pleasing sound;
I grant I never saw a goddess go –
My mistress when she walks, treads on the ground.
  And yet, by heaven, I think my love as rare
  As any she belied with false compare.

Second wives

Your love did not find us vertical
and rotating around a dance hall,
or chaperoned on an afternoon lawn

pretending to read. We earned it
like our money, angled over desks,
over your children, comforted you

down corridors. And if you never tore
an evening dress we wore, you never
had to bolt the door against us

while we accepted you maimed,
the family seat razed to the ground;
that book you kept with grass-stained pages.

Thomas Wyatt

'Whoso list to hunt'

Whoso list to hunt, I know where is an hind,
But as for me, helas, I may no more.
The vain travail hath wearied me so sore,
I am of them that farthest cometh behind.
Yet may I by no means my wearied mind
Draw from the deer, but as she fleeth afore
Fainting I follow. I leave off therefore
Sithens in a net I seek to hold the wind.
Who list her hunt, I put him out of doubt,
As well as I may spend his time in vain.
And graven with diamonds in letters plain
There is written her fair neck round about:
'*Noli me tangere* for Caesar's I am,
And wild for to hold though I seem tame.'

Bloody Men

Bloody men are like bloody buses –
You wait for about a year
And as soon as one approaches your stop
Two or three others appear.

You look at them flashing their indicators,
Offering you a ride.
You're trying to read the destinations,
You haven't much time to decide.

If you make a mistake, there is no turning back.
Jump off, and you'll stand there and gaze
While the cars and the taxis and lorries go by
And the minutes, the hours, the days.

Never the Time and the Place

Never the time and the place
    And the loved one all together!
This path – how soft to pace!
    This May – what magic weather!
    Where is the loved one's face?
In a dream that loved one's face meets mine,
    But the house is narrow, the place is bleak
Where, outside, rain and wind combine
    With a furtive ear, if I strive to speak,
    With hostile eye at my flushing cheek,
With a malice that marks each word, each sign!
O enemy sly and serpentine,
    Uncoil thee from the waking man!
        Do I hold the Past
        Thus firm and fast
    Yet doubt if the Future hold I can?
This path so soft to pace shall lead
Thro' the magic of May to herself indeed!
Or narrow if needs the house must be,
Outside are the storms and strangers: we—
Oh, close, safe, warm sleep I and she,
—I and she!

Funeral Blues

Stop all the clocks, cut off the telephone,
Prevent the dog from barking with a juicy bone,
Silence the pianos and with muffled drum
Bring out the coffin, let the mourners come.

Let aeroplanes circle moaning overhead
Scribbling on the sky the message He Is Dead,
Put crepe bows round the white necks of the public doves,
Let the traffic policemen wear black cotton gloves.

He was my North, my South, my East and West,
My working week and my Sunday rest,
My noon, my midnight, my talk, my song;
I thought that love would last for ever: I was wrong.

The stars are not wanted now: put out every one;
Pack up the moon and dismantle the sun;
Pour away the ocean and sweep up the wood.
For nothing now can ever come to any good.

Walsingham

'As you came from the holy land
    Of Walsingham,
Met you not with my true love
    By the way as you came?'

'How shall I know your true love,
    That have met many one
As I went to the holy land,
    That have come, that have gone?'

'She is neither white nor brown,
    But as the heavens fair,
There is none hath a form so divine
    In the earth or the air.'

'Such an one did I meet, good Sir,
    Such an angelic face,
Who like a queen, like a nymph did appear
    By her gait, by her grace.'

'She hath left me here all alone,
    All alone as unknown,
Who sometimes did me lead with herself,
    And me loved as her own.'

'What's the cause that she leaves you alone
    And a new way doth take,
Who loved you once as her own
    And her joy did you make?'

'I have loved her all my youth,
　　But now old as you see,
Love likes not the falling fruit
　　From the withered tree.

'Know that Love is a careless child,
　　And forgets promise past;
He is blind, he is deaf when he list
　　And in faith never fast.

'His desire is a dureless content
　　And a trustless joy;
He is won with a world of despair
　　And is lost with a toy.

'Of womenkind such indeed is the love
　　Or the word love abused,
Under which many childish desires
　　And conceits are excused.

'But true Love is a durable fire
　　In the mind ever burning;
Never sick, never old, never dead,
　　From itself never turning.'

For My Lover, Returning to His Wife

She is all there.
She was melted carefully down for you
and cast up from your childhood,
cast up from your one hundred favorite aggies.

She has always been there, my darling.
She is, in fact, exquisite.
Fireworks in the dull middle of February
and as real as a cast-iron pot.

Let's face it, I have been momentary.
A luxury. A bright red sloop in the harbor.
My hair rising like smoke from the car window.
Littleneck clams out of season.

She is more than that. She is your have to have,
has grown you your practical your tropical growth.
This is not an experiment. She is all harmony.
She sees to oars and oarlocks for the dinghy,

has placed wild flowers at the window at breakfast,
sat by the potter's wheel at midday,
set forth three children under the moon,
three cherubs drawn by Michelangelo,

done this with her legs spread out
in the terrible months in the chapel.
If you glance up, the children are there
like delicate balloons resting on the ceiling.

She has also carried each one down the hall
after supper, their heads privately bent,
two legs protesting, person to person,
her face flushed with a song and their little sleep.

I give you back your heart.
I give you permission —

for the fuse inside her, throbbing
angrily in the dirt, for the bitch in her
and the burying of her wound —
for the burying of her small red wound alive —

for the pale flickering flare under her ribs,
for the drunken sailor who waits in her left pulse,
for the mother's knee, for the stockings,
for the garter belt, for the call —

the curious call
when you will burrow in arms and breasts
and tug at the orange ribbon in her hair
and answer the call, the curious call.

She is so naked and singular.
She is the sum of yourself and your dream.
Climb her like a monument, step after step.
She is solid.

As for me, I am a watercolor.
I wash off.

'When I have fears that I may cease to be'

When I have fears that I may cease to be
  Before my pen has gleaned my teeming brain,
Before high-pilèd books, in charactery,
  Hold like rich garners the full-ripened grain;
When I behold, upon the night's starred face,
  Huge cloudy symbols of a high romance,
And think that I may never live to trace
  Their shadows, with the magic hand of chance;
And when I feel, fair creature of an hour!
  That I shall never look upon thee more,
Never have relish in the faery power,
  Of unreflecting love! – then on the shore
Of the wide world I stand alone, and think
Till love and fame to nothingness do sink.

Tonight I Can Write

Tonight I can write the saddest lines.

Write, for example, 'The night is shattered
and the blue stars shiver in the distance.'

The night wind revolves in the sky and sings.

Tonight I can write the saddest lines.
I loved her, and sometimes she loved me too.

Through nights like this one I held her in my arms.
I kissed her again and again under the endless sky.

She loved me, sometimes I loved her too.
How could one not have loved her great still eyes.

Tonight I can write the saddest lines.
To think that I do not have her. To feel that I have lost her.

To hear the immense night, still more immense without her.
And the verse falls to the soul like dew to the pasture.

What does it matter that my love could not keep her.
The night is shattered and she is not with me.

This is all. In the distance someone is singing. In the distance.
My soul is not satisfied that it has lost her.

My sight searches for her as though to go to her.
My heart looks for her, and she is not with me.

The same night whitening the same trees.
We, of that time, are no longer the same.

I no longer love her, that's certain, but how I loved her.
My voice tried to find the wind to touch her hearing.

Another's. She will be another's. Like my kisses before.
Her voice. Her bright body. Her infinite eyes.

I no longer love her, that's certain, but maybe I love her.
Love is so short, forgetting is so long.

Because through nights like this one I held her in my arms
my soul is not satisfied that it has lost her.

Though this be the last pain that she makes me suffer
and these the last verses that I write for her.

trans. W. S. Merwin

Exile

For Conal Holmes O'Connell O'Riordan

By the sad waters of separation
    Where we have wandered by divers ways,
I have but the shadow and imitation
    Of the old memorial days.

In music I have no consolation,
    No roses are pale enough for me;
The sound of the waters of separation
    Surpasseth roses and melody.

By the sad waters of separation
    Dimly I hear from an hidden place
The sigh of mine ancient adoration:
    Hardly can I remember your face.

If you be dead, no proclamation
    Sprang to me over the waste, gray sea.
Living, the waters of separation
    Sever for ever your soul from me.

No man knoweth our desolation;
    Memory pales of the old delight;
While the sad waters of separation
    Bear us on to the ultimate night.

Michael Donaghy

Reprimands

We fell out of love as toddlers fall
glancing down, distracted, at their feet,
as the pianist in the concert hall
betrays her hands to thought and adds an extra
beat –
The thought vertiginous. The reprimand.
It fells the bee mid-flight. It made me stall
before a holy water font in Rome
half afraid that if I dipped my hand
I'd find the water's surface hard as stone
and – this you'd never understand –
half afraid to leave the thing alone.
For I'd been taught that Jesus walked the sea
and came to Peter three leagues out of port.
Said Peter *Bid me to come unto thee*
and strode on faith dryfoot until he thought . . .
and thinking, sank, I'd never learnt to swim
but I'd seen insects skim across a pond
and I'd seen glasses filled above the brim.
Some firm conviction keeps a raindrop round.
What kept me rigid as a mannequin?
We fell out of love and nearly drowned.
The very wordlessness all lovers want
to feel beneath their feet like solid ground
dissolved to silences no human shout
could ripple –
                    like the surface of that font
when other voices, tourist and devout,
grew still, and someone whispered by my side

O ye of little faith – and shallow doubt –
choose here to wet that hand or stand aside.
No one was there. But I could tell that tone.
I heard his ancient apostolic voice
this evening when I went to lift the phone
to tell you this – and froze. The reprimand.
For once, in two minds, Thomas made the choice
to bless and wet with blood his faithless hand.

Thomas Wyatt

'They flee from me that sometime did me seek'

They flee from me that sometime did me seek,
　With naked foot stalking in my chamber.
I have seen them gentle, tame and meek,
　That now are wild and do not remember
　That sometime they put themselves in danger
　　To take bread at my hand; and now they range
　　Busily seeking with a continual change.

Thankt be fortune, it hath been otherwise
　Twenty times better; but once, in special
In thin array, after a pleasant guise,
　When her loose gown from her shoulders did fall,
　And she me caught in her arms long and small,
　　There with all sweetly did me kiss,
　　And softly said: 'Dear heart, how like you this?'

It was no dream; I lay broad waking:
　But all is turned thorough my gentleness
Into a strange fashion of forsaking;
　And I have leave to go of her goodness;
　And she also to use new-fangleness.
　　But since that I so kindly am served,
　　I fain would know what she hath deserved.

Badly-Chosen Lover

Criminal, you took a great piece of my life,
And you took it under false pretences,
That piece of time
– In the clear muscles of my brain
I have the lens and jug of it!
Books, thoughts, meals, days, and houses,
Half Europe, spent like a coarse banknote,
You took it – leaving mud and cabbage stumps.

And, Criminal, I damn you for it (very softly).
My spirit broke her fast on you. And, Turk,
You fed her with the breath of your neck
– In my brain's clear retina
I have the stolen love-behaviour.
Your heart, greedy and tepid, brothel-meat,
Gulped it, like a flunkey with erotica.
And very softly, Criminal, I *damn* you for it.

Arracombe Wood

Some said, because he wud'n spaik
Any words to women but Yes and No,
Nor put out his hand for Parson to shake
He mun be bird-witted. But I do go
By the lie of the barley that he did sow,
And I wish no better thing than to hold a rake
Like Dave, in his time, or to see him mow.

Put up in churchyard a month ago,
"A bitter old soul," they said, but it wadn't so.
His heart were in Arracombe Wood where he'd used to go
To sit and talk wi' his shadder till sun went low,
Though what it was all about us'll never know.
And there baint no mem'ry in the place
Of th' old man's footmark, nor his face;
Arracombe Wood do think more of a crow—
'Will be violets there in the Spring: in Summer time the spider's lace;
And come the Fall, the whizzle and race
Of the dry, dead leaves when the wind gies chase;
And on the Eve of Christmas, fallin' snow.

Lone Gentleman

Young homosexuals and girls in love,
and widows gone to seed, sleepless, delirious,
and novice housewives pregnant some thirty hours,
the hoarse cats cruising across my garden's shadows
like a necklace of throbbing, sexual oysters
surround my solitary home
like enemies entrenched against my soul,
like conspirators in pyjamas
exchanging long, thick kisses on the sly.

The radiant summer entices lovers here
in melancholic regiments
made up of fat and flabby, gay and mournful couples:
under the graceful palm trees, along the moonlit beach,
there is a continual excitement of trousers and petticoats,
the crisp sound of stockings caressed,
women's breasts shining like eyes.

It's quite clear that the local clerk, bored to the hilt,
after his weekday tedium, cheap paperbacks in bed,
has managed to make his neighbour
and he takes her to the miserable flea-pits
where the heroes are young stallions or passionate princes:
he caresses her legs downy with soft hair
with his wet, hot hands smelling of cigarillos.

Seducers' afternoons and strictly legal nights
fold together like a pair of sheets, burying me:
the siesta hours when young male and female students
as well as priests retire to masturbate,
and when animals screw outright,
and bees smell of blood and furious flies buzz,
and cousins play kinkily with their girl cousins,
and doctors glare angrily at their young patient's husband,
and the professor, almost unconsciously, during the morning hours,
copes with his marital duties and then has breakfast,
and, later on, the adulterers who love each other with real love,
on beds as high and spacious as sea-going ships –
so for sure and for ever this great forest surrounds me,
breathing through flowers large as mouths chock full of teeth,
black-rooted in the shapes of hoofs and shoes.

trans. Nathaniel Tarn

Sonnet 73

That time of year thou mayst in me behold
When yellow leaves, or none, or few, do hang
Upon those boughs which shake against the cold,
Bare ruin'd choirs where late the sweet birds sang.
In me thou seest the twilight of such day
As after sunset fadeth in the west,
Which by and by black night doth take away,
Death's second self, that seals up all in rest.
In me thou seest the glowing of such fire
That on the ashes of his youth doth lie,
As the death-bed whereon it must expire,
Consum'd by that which it was nourished by.
  This thou perceiv'st which makes thy love more strong,
  To love that well which thou must leave ere long.

ZSUZSA RAKOVSZKY

They Were Burning Dead Leaves

They were burning dead leaves. Must oozed with scent,
    tar bubbled and blew.
The moonlight glow behind the thistle bent
    like a torn rainbow.

The street was a forest, night slid into the heart
    of deepest autumn.
A guilty music blew the house apart
    with its fife and drum.

To have this again, just this, just the once more:
    I would sink below
autumnal earth and place my right hand in your
    hand like a shadow.

trans. George Szirtes

He Wishes for the Cloths of Heaven

Had I the heavens' embroidered cloths,
Enwrought with golden and silver light,
The blue and the dim and the dark cloths
Of night and light and the half-light,
I would spread the cloths under your feet:
But I, being poor, have only my dreams;
I have spread my dreams under your feet;
Tread softly because you tread on my dreams.

Feathers

With the woman from your office that you left her for
away at a weekend conference, you found yourself
at a party staring at your ex-girlfriend and her
new boyfriend, and deciding that the new boyfriend's
jumper was the kind favoured by train spotters or
watchers of birds (the sort that fly without any help
from you) repaired to the bedroom set aside for coats,
got as close as you could to the dressing-table mirror,
and practised saying *For old times' sake* with your eyes.

But you didn't know that on the evenings you were
working late, she had put off going home to an empty flat
by browsing in a bookshop near the station, and read
in the poetry section that hope is the thing with feathers
and in the natural world section that ninety per cent
of bird species are monogamous compared with
three per cent of mammals, and bought herself a pocket
guide by Bill Oddie and binoculars one lunchtime from a
sports shop, and waited for the day when you would leave.

So when you approached her at the buffet table
your 'come to bed' look didn't register and you found
yourself demanding *Who's the fucking jumper?*

Refilling their glasses in the kitchen her new boyfriend
picked up that stunned silence in which he could have
told you about the day on Hackney Marsh
when from his hide he saw her walking towards him,
a new variety that he couldn't name, who wanted to learn
everything he could teach her and had him describe swans
mating for life again and again and again, and how much
she loves his jumpers, particularly this one,
bought by her and worn by him to repel birds of prey.

EDWARD THOMAS

When We Two Walked

WHEN we two walked in Lent
We imagined that happiness
Was something different
And this was something less.

But happy were we to hide
Our happiness, not as they were
Who acted in their pride
Juno and Jupiter:

For the Gods in their jealousy
Murdered that wife and man.
And we that were wise live free
To recall our happiness then.

Watching Young Couples with an Old Girlfriend on Sunday Morning

How mild these young men seem to me now
with their baggy shorts and clouds of musk,
as if younger brothers of the women they escort
in tight black leather, bangs and tattoos,
cute little toughies, so Louise Brooks annealed

in MTV, headed off for huevos rancheros
and the Sunday *Times* at some chic, crowded dive.
I don't recall it at all this way, do you?
How sweetly complected and confident they look,
their faces unclouded by the rages

and abandoned, tearful couplings of the night before,
the drunkenness, beast savor and remorse.
Or do I recoil from their youthfulness and health?
Oh, not recoil, just fail to see ourselves.
And yet, this tenderness between us that remains

was mortared first with a darkness that got loose, a frenzy,
we still, we still refuse to name.

Thomas Campion

'When thou must home to shades of under ground'

When thou must home to shades of under ground,
And there arriv'd a new admired guest,
The beauteous spirits do engirt thee round,
White Iope, blith Hellen, and the rest,
To hear the stories of thy finisht love
From that smooth tongue whose music hell can move;

Then wilt thou speak of banqueting delights,
Of masks and revels which sweet youth did make,
Of tourneys and great challenges of knights,
And all these triumphs for thy beauty's sake:
When thou hast told these honours done to thee,
Then tell, O tell, how thou didst murder me.

Campionesque for Anna

When I lay down where I had lain with you
Some many nights, beloved, of the days
Lit by your sun, I dreamed all touch untrue,
Error my star and darkness all my ways
Till where I lay, I lay again with you.

Till where I go, I go again with you
Through all the days, beloved, and the nights
By your sweet self illumined, I can do
Not one good thing: not till your beauty lights
Me where I go, and go again with you.

WILLIAM BARNES

'With you first shown to me'

With you first shown to me,
With you first known to me,
My life-time loom'd, in hope, a length of joy
Your voice so sweetly spoke,
Your mind so meetly spoke,
My hopes were all of bliss without alloy,
As I, for your abode, sought out, with pride,
This house with vines o'er-ranging all its side.

I thought of years to come,
All free of tears to come,
When I might call you mine, and mine alone,
With steps to fall for me,
And day cares all for me,
And hands for ever nigh to help my own;
And then thank'd Him who had not cast my time
Too early or too late for your sweet prime.

Then bright was dawn, o'er dew,
And day withdrawn, o'er dew,
And mid-day glow'd on flow'rs along the ledge,
And walls in sight, afar,
Were shining white, afar,
And brightly shone the stream beside the sedge.
But still, the fairest light of those clear days
Seem'd that which fell along your flow'ry ways.

Sally Somewhere

doesn't know where:
she lifts the carpet and squints through the floor
    at dusty joists, old nails and hair;
she opens oranges and searches their quarters,
    frays her hems, unpicks her seams,
holds each dress up before a Maglite beam,
    scanning for shadows, outlines, stains.
She unscrews the U-bend and six Parker pens,
    spreads the ink out with her fingers,
explores its consistency, checks its borders,
    then finds her own hands are hidden from her.
She dislodges the cistern's white porcelain lid
    then climbs the ladder up to the attic,
where she frisks the immersion heater's red padded jacket.
    Washing-line, sink-side, bedside;
clear-sided cyclonic Dyson's insides she tries:
    nothing. She shakes each shoe,
peels each black boot from its tube of air,
    sifts flour, tests temperatures, weights;
she measures, she meters, clocks water rates,
    candle-lengths, matchstick and page numbers,
counts between lightning crack and first roll of thunder,
    then pencils the data
in diaries and maths books, on blue-gridded paper.
    She asks me. I couldn't tell her.
She kicks through leaves, looks down light-shafts; she thinks
    the flattened grass is a clue to what rested
then took off, got taken apart or rolled past
    while she slept. She's vexed; she's pestered;

won't let it arrive when it chooses, won't stop
    combing the head of the rag-haired mop
or winding the taps like the crowns of a watch.
    I say: Don't you know what you've got?

The Wife a-Lost

Since I noo mwore do zee your feäce,
   Up steärs or down below,
I'll zit me in the lwonesome pleäce,
   Where flat-bough'd beech do grow:
Below the beeches' bough, my love,
   Where you did never come,
An' I don't look to meet ye now,
   As I do look at hwome.

Since you noo mwore be at my zide,
   In walks in zummer het,
I'll goo alwone where mist do ride,
   Drough trees a-drippen wet:
Below the raïn-wet bough, my love,
   Where you did never come,
An' I don't grieve to miss ye now,
   As I do grieve at hwome.

Since now bezide my dinner-bwoard
   Your vaïce do never sound,
I'll eat the bit I can avword,
   A-vield upon the ground;
Below the darksome bough, my love,
   Where you did never dine,
An' I don't grieve to miss ye now,
   As I at hwome do pine.

Since I do miss your vaïce an' feäce
   In präyer at eventide,
I'll präy wi oone sad vaïce vor greäce
   To goo where you do bide;
Above the tree an' bough, my love,
   Where you be gone avore,
An' be a-waïten vor me now,
   To come vor evermwore.

You Hated Spain

Spain frightened you. Spain
Where I felt at home. The blood-raw light,
The oiled anchovy faces, the African
Black edges to everything, frightened you.
Your schooling had somehow neglected Spain.
The wrought-iron grille, death and the Arab drum.
You did not know the language, your soul was empty
Of the signs, and the welding light
Made your blood shrivel. Bosch
Held out a spidery hand and you took it
Timidly, a bobby-sox American.
You saw right down to the Goya funeral grin
And recognized it, and recoiled
As your poems winced into chill, as your panic
Clutched back towards college America.
So we sat as tourists at the bullfight
Watching bewildered bulls awkwardly butchered,
Seeing the grey-faced matador, at the barrier
Just below us, straightening his bent sword
And vomiting with fear. And the horn
That hid itself inside the blowfly belly
Of the toppled picador punctured
What was waiting for you. Spain
Was the land of your dreams: the dust-red cadaver
You dared not wake with, the puckering amputations
No literature course had glamorized.
The juju land behind your African lips.
Spain was what you tried to wake up from
And could not. I see you, in moonlight,

Walking the empty wharf at Alicante
Like a soul waiting for the ferry,
A new soul, still not understanding,
Thinking it is still your honeymoon
In the happy world, with your whole life waiting,
Happy, and all your poems still to be found.

Love and Life

All my past life is mine no more;
   The flying hours are gone,
Like transitory dreams given o'er
Whose images are kept in store
   By memory alone.

Whatever is to come is not:
   How can it then be mine?
The present moment's all my lot,
And that, as fast as it is got,
   Phyllis, is wholly thine.

Then talk not of inconstancy,
   False hearts, and broken vows;
If I, by miracle, can be
This livelong minute true to thee,
   'Tis all that heaven allows.

PAUL MULDOON

Long Finish

Ten years since we were married, since we stood
under a chuppah of pine boughs
in the middle of a little pinewood
and exchanged our wedding vows.
Save me, good thou,
a piece of marchpane, while I fill your glass with Simi
Chardonnay as high as decency allows,
and then some.

Bear with me now as I myself must bear
the scrutiny of a bottle of wine
that boasts of hints of plum and pear,
its muscadine
tempered by an oak backbone. I myself have designs
on the willow-boss
of your breast, on all your waist confines
between longing and loss.

The wonder is that we somehow have withstood
the soars and slumps in the Dow
of ten years of marriage and parenthood,
its summits and its sloughs—
that we've somehow
managed to withstand an almond-blossomy
five years of bitter rapture, five of blissful rows
(and then some,

if we count the one or two to spare
when we've been firmly on cloud nine).
Even now, as you turn away from me with your one bare
shoulder, the veer of your neckline,
I glimpse the all-but-cleared-up eczema patch on your spine
and it brings to mind not the Schloss
that stands, transitory, tra la, Triestine,
between longing and loss

but a crude
hip-trench in a field, covered with pine boughs,
in which two men in masks and hoods
who have themselves taken vows
wait for a farmer to break a bale for his cows
before opening fire with semi-
automatics, cutting him off slightly above the eyebrows,
and then some.

It brings to mind another, driving out to care
for six white-faced kine
finishing on heather and mountain air,
another who'll shortly divine
the precise whereabouts of a landmine
on the road between Beragh and Sixmilecross,
who'll shortly know what it is to have breasted the line
between longing and loss.

Such forbearance in the face of vicissitude
also brings to mind the little 'there, there's and 'now, now's
of two sisters whose sleeves are imbued
with the constant douse and souse
of salt-water through their salt-house
in *Matsukaze* (or 'Pining Wind'), by Zeami,
the salt-house through which the wind soughs and soughs,
and then some

of the wind's little 'now, now's and 'there, there's
seem to intertwine
with those of Pining Wind and Autumn Rain, who must forbear
the dolor of their lives of boiling down brine.
For the double meaning of 'pine'
is much the same in Japanese as English, coming across
both in the sense of 'tree' and the sense we assign
between 'longing' and 'loss'

as when the ghost of Yukihira, the poet-courtier who wooed
both sisters, appears as a ghostly pine, pining among pine boughs.
Barely have Autumn Rain and Pining Wind renewed their vows
than you turn back towards me and your blouse,
while it covers the all-but-cleared-up patch of eczema,
falls as low as decency allows,
and then some.

Princess of Accutane, let's no more try to refine
the pure drop from the dross
than distinguish, good thou, between mine and thine,
between longing and loss,
but rouse
ourselves each dawn, here on the shore at Suma,
with such force and fervor as spouses may yet espouse,
and then some.

'Now sleeps the crimson petal, now the white'

Now sleeps the crimson petal, now the white;
Nor waves the cypress in the palace walk;
Nor winks the gold fin in the porphyry font:
The firefly wakens: waken thou with me.

Now droops the milk-white peacock like a ghost,
And like a ghost she glimmers on to me.

Now lies the Earth all Danaë to the stars,
And all thy heart lies open unto me.

Now slides the silent meteor on, and leaves
A shining furrow, as thy thoughts in me.

Now folds the lily all her sweetness up,
And slips into the bosom of the lake:
So fold thyself, my dearest, thou, and slip
Into my bosom and be lost in me.

Yeah Yeah Yeah

No matter what you did to her, she said,
There's times, she said, she misses you, your face
Will pucker in her dream, and times the bed's
Too big. Stray hairs will surface in a place
You used to leave your shoes. A certain phrase,
Some old song on the radio, a joke
You had to be there for, she said, some days
It really gets to her; the way you smoked
Or held a cup, or her, and how you woke
Up crying in the night sometimes, the way
She'd stroke and hush you back, and how you broke
Her still. All this she told me yesterday,
Then she rolled over, laughed, began to do
To me what she so rarely did with you.

'Since there's no help, come let us kiss and part'

Since there's no help, come let us kiss and part;
Nay, I have done, you get no more of me,
And I am glad, yea, glad with all my heart
That thus so cleanly I myself can free;
Shake hands for ever, cancel all our vows,
And when we meet at any time again,
Be it not seen in either of our brows
That we one jot of former love retain.
Now at the last gasp of Love's latest breath,
When, his pulse failing, Passion speechless lies,
When Faith is kneeling by his bed of death,
And Innocence is closing up his eyes,
    Now if thou wouldst, when all have given him over,
    From death to life thou mightst him yet recover.

Slattern

I leave myself about, slatternly,
bits of me, and times I liked:
I let them go on lying where
they fall, crumple, if they will,
I know fine how to make them walk
and breathe again. Sometimes at night,
or on the train, I dream I'm dancing,
or lying in someone's arms who says
he loves my eyes in French, and again
and again I am walking up your road,
that first time, bidden and wanted,
the blossom on the trees, light,
light and buoyant. *Pull yourself
together*, they say, quite rightly,
but she is stubborn, that girl,
that hopeful one, still walking.

On His Mistress Drowned

Sweet stream, that doth with equal pace
  Both thy self fly, and thy self chase
    Forbear awhile to flow,
    And listen to my woe.

Then go, and tell the sea that all its brine
  Is fresh, compar'd to mine;
Inform it that the gentler dame,
Who was the life of all my flame,
  In the glory of her bud,
  Has pass'd the fatal flood,
Death by this only stroke triumphs above
  The greatest power of love :
  Alas, alas! I must give o'er,
My sighs will let me add no more.
  Go on, sweet stream, and henceforth rest,
No more than does my troubled breast;
And if my sad complaints have made thee stay,
  These tears, these tears shall mend thy way.

KIT WRIGHT

Letter to Anna, Pregnant

When I consider
By the frozen river
How we two shall never
Down some of these days
Meet in loving
Upon the ungrieving
Bank in forgiving
New-made rays

Of April sunlight
When touch is leaf-light
And love is outright
And darkness done,
Then I remember
Times without number
The cold I shouldered
To block your sun.

And I apportion,
By this sad station
Where ice to the ocean
Flows downstream,
All blame attendant
To your correspondent,
Sorrow his tenant,
Drowned that dream.

The hawthorn crouches
In the black wind's clutches
And snags and scratches
The last of light
That is dying over
The winter river
That sails forever
On out of sight.

I'm sorry, darling,
I hope the unfurling
Bud in your sailing
Body may
Beyond shores woeful
Wake you joyful,
Wake you joyful
Some sweet day.

The Love Song

Out of the blackthorn edges
I caught a tune
And before it could vanish, seized
It, wrote it down.

Gave to a girl, so praising
Her eyes, lips and hair
She had little knowing, it was only thorn
Had dreamed of a girl there.

Prettily she thanked me, and never
Guessed any of my deceit . . .
But O Earth is this the only way
Man may conquer, a girl surrender her sweet?

Static

The storm shakes out its sheets
against the darkening window:
the glass flinches under thrown hail.
Unhinged, the television slips its hold,
Streams into black and white
then silence, as the lines go down.
Her postcards stir on the shelf, tip over;
the lights of Calais trip out one by one.

He cannot tell her
how the geese scull back at twilight,
how the lighthouse walks its beam
across the trenches of the sea.
He cannot tell her how the open night
swings like a door without her,
how he is the lock
and she is the key.

W. B. YEATS

No Second Troy

Why should I blame her that she filled my days
With misery, or that she would of late
Have taught to ignorant men most violent ways,
Or hurled the little streets upon the great,
Had they but courage equal to desire?
What could have made her peaceful with a mind
That nobleness made simple as a fire,
With beauty like a tightened bow, a kind
That is not natural in an age like this,
Being high and solitary and most stern?
Why, what could she have done, being what she is?
Was there another Troy for her to burn?

The Serpent Beguiled Me

Following Eve, you look for apple cores
Along the riverbank, tossed in the mud.
Following Adam down long corridors,
You swing your torch to look for spit and blood.

He got his chest condition when he learned
Contentment made her curious. He thought
He was enough for her, and what he earned
Would keep her pinned while he played covert sport.

Alas, not so. She claimed that privilege too,
And even, under wraps, nursed the same pride
In taking satiation as her due—
A cue to call herself dissatisfied.

That rate of change was coded by the tree
Into the fruit. The instant thrill of sin
Turned sweet release to bitter urgency:
His fig leaf was flicked off, and hers sucked in.

From that day forth, the syrup she gave down
Smacked of the knowledge that she felt no shame.
The modesty for which she won renown
Was feigned to keep her freedom free of blame.

There was a time when, if he had not worn
Her out, she would have lain awake and wept.
Why was the truth, we ask, so slow to dawn?
He should have guessed it from how well she slept.

And when she turned to him, as she did still,
Though the old compulsion was no longer there,
The readiness with which she drank her fill
Told him in vain her fancy lay elsewhere.

He never faced the fact until she went.
He tracked her down and asked her what was wrong.
For once she said exactly what she meant:
'It was perfect. It just went on too long.'

Envoy

Vitae summa brevis spem nos vetat incohare longam

They are not long, the weeping and the laughter,
    Love and desire and hate:
I think they have no portion in us after
      We pass the gate.

They are not long, the days of wine and roses:
    Out of a misty dream
Our path emerges for a while, then closes
      Within a dream.

Closure

'You never really know why you've made the mistakes you've made until you've lived through all their consequences.'
— Daniel in *La Porte Grise Ouverte* (dir. de-Vette, 1968)

5.10 p.m.

She pours down the phone at me, sobs,
'John, what's going on? *John!'*
'I'm in a callbox,' I say, 'I locked myself out –
yes, *locked,* yes, *out.'*

11.00 a.m.

I describe a parabola with the ball of my left foot
on his living-room carpet.
I've been caught in the company of uncool friends:
the clinging tracksuit bottoms,
the companionable tea-stained jumper,
trainers like lolling dogs' tongues.
'Taking out the rubbish,' I say.
'I can see it now: the tug, the slam.
It pulled the doormat right out from under me.
And you know that place is like a sealed box
I don't think Houdini could get himself into.
But she's bound to be back sooner or later.'
He says, 'We'll go to the movies.'

9.20 a.m.

I am holding my parents, they are split
in two separate photographs in a box frame.
They each sit in a wicker basket seat at Kenwood
with their easy fifties smiles.
They have taken turns in that same seat
for these Box Brownie snaps,
but I have placed them side by side
after all that elapsing.
A couple of adulterers in the making,
they grin back at the camera.
If they could see beyond it,
past the temporary trees of a particular July day,
if their eyes could focus past the sunshine that strikes them
precisely at the speed of light,
see through all that hocus-pocus,
they would see that they are looking straight at me,
for once not trying to shake off the feeling
that they are beautiful fools,
wedded to the course of events
that flicks up images which appear static
because caught between blinks.
I mouth a habitual prayer to understand.
        They peer back,
turn to one another, he speaks:

'Look at him, always so quick to jump to delusions.'
'What about the tears and rages,
the torn-up love notes, the early deaths?'
'Our lives killed us, everyone's do – he should be careful.'
'Tell him that.'
'Just shut the bedroom door, boy, and enjoy the day.
Look at us . . . and we've been dead these twenty years.'

They turn back to that Eden of gardens,
the fixative seeping away over the years.
I clatter the contents of my pockets from the bedside
and replace it with their photos.

2.15 p.m.

We go and see the new Tarantino with its addiction
to jump-cut technique: time sliced up
as if it were nothing so much as a backdrop,
a prop to be wheeled on whenever,
time, like a worn-out old actor from the forties
who once slept with Rita Hayworth,
but who is now just grateful for a cameo as a gutter drunk.
'Who's Rita Hayworth?' asks the key grip.

9.15 a.m.

I run my hands over and over my poems,
lay them all out on the bed.
I am given up to these secret lyrics.
Through them I enter that reversed zone
between the silver and the mirror
where the clock runs backwards to time
and I act out absurdist soliloquies of lost love.
I think I can keep it all separate, hold it all apart,
keep it in me, in the poetry. In the living room,
Otis Redding's alive and intoning;
the mortal timbre of his voice takes its toll.
I glance across at my parents smiling out into the light,
go over and clasp them in my hands.

8.45 a.m.

The kitchen reeks of stale compromise
and unpalatable accommodations. She eggs
me on to cross knives with her. I don't.
If I could work up the appetite
we wouldn't be here,
facing into the face of each other,
in the first place.
      You can hear the hiss
of our brand new Russell Hobbs;
the chords ascend sibilantly: the fourth, the fifth.
      In the name of all that's nameless,
she accuses me of an affair.
She doesn't know the reason I never could
isn't because I don't feel that cold nausea for it,
the grope at breath that at some party
my mouth is going to say 'I was just wondering . . .'
and I'm *married*. No, none of it –
my parents, they made me this way.
      I catch myself in the kettle's chrome:
a tiny bulbous shape puzzling at itself.
The steam rises like ectoplasm;
something is leaving its earthly form.
      I hold my breath
in this locked, chained and buckled box
submerged in six foot of dirty dishwater;
my lungs are shot and I'm gagging.
I should clarify: my body remains stuck fast
to the seat-vinyl of the kitchen chair,
but someone in me, someone I'd forgotten I even knew,
decides to make a clean break for it, to take charge and say:
this is it, we're leaving, no more of this shit,
nothing, nil, nought, nix;

say goodbye to Manderley;
Grab your coat and get your hat . . .
It's then I hear my own voice saying:
'Let's just give it a little more time . . .'
Exit wife from flat, at this point.

2.35 p.m.

My friend sits with a silo of popcorn on his knee –
he's from America; they do things differently there –
he erupts in white froth at the film.
It's as if there's not enough effervescence on the screen.
Perhaps it excites some awful froth need in him
as we watch Travolta resurrect himself
with automatic handguns and heroin,
see the horrible ifs accumulate, the stiffs agglomerate,
the action roll itself backwards
to where Pumpkin and Honey Bunny get let off with their lives,
the one place in the film that will do for a happy ending.
As if that would be, or as if there's something awry
with unhappy endings, things finished,
something completing its rightful term,
coming down to no more than a memory,
some love songs and a couple of old photographs.

5.15 p.m.

Back in the phone-booth and she's still screaming,
still screaming about 'these poems',
'these poems about this woman, this (she says *her* name).
Who is she, John? What's going on?'
In a few frames the day folds up around me

like a cheap car in a crash,
concertinas bit by bit in slow-mo,
a scrunching French kiss; it all rushes at me:
the photoframe, the popcorn, the poems.
'I'll come straight home,' I say. 'I'll explain.'
But I don't want to explain:
it's all there on the bed.

   10.13 a.m.

It's that morning and I'm outside the flat;
the bin bags are there in front of me,
as are John Travolta and the misplaced keys,
the poetry, the phone box and the end,
when I turn, with nothing in my head
but the dead vowels of Otis Redding,
lost love and getting shot of the rubbish,
stretch out my arm for the front door and see it closing.

To the Virgins, to Make Much of Time

Gather ye rosebuds while ye may,
   Old time is still a-flying:
And this same flower that smiles today
   Tomorrow will be dying.

The glorious lamp of heaven, the sun,
   The higher he's a-getting,
The sooner will his race be run,
   And nearer he's to setting.

That age is best which is the first,
   When youth and blood are warmer;
But being spent, the worse, and worst
   Times still succeed the former.

Then be not coy, but use your time,
   And while ye may, go marry:
For having lost but once your prime
   You may for ever tarry.

Indian Summer

these iron comforts, reasonable taboos
– John Ashbery

Look at this frosty red rose leaning over
The milk on the step. Please take it. But leave me
Its fragrance, its ice in the mind, to remember you by.
The girlfriends of afternoon drinkers
(*O the criminal classes, their bottle-tanned lasses*)
Have locked up their halters and shorts –
Being practical girls, they have understood soon
What I struggle with late, getting grit in my eyes –
That the piss-palace garden is windy and dim
When the heat goes at four. It is over again.
Now the engineer turns up to service the heating
And says: *I see your bell's still bust*
From the Charon-cold depths of his anorak hood.
The dark house is a coffin of laws; early closing.
But if the clocks must forever go back
To the meantime of Pluto, leave me your voice,
Its rumour at the confluence of Portugal and Spain,
From whose entwining waters rises, like a shell
Within the echo in the ear, your own supreme Creole.
If I am doomed to winter on the Campo Mediocrita
Whose high plateau becomes the windy shore
Of an ocean with only one side, to wait
Where the howling sunshine does not warm me,
Let me speak your tongue, at least –
For yours is the music the panther laments in,
Retreating to Burradon, yours is the silvery

Script of the spider at midnight,
Your diary is scandal's pleasure-ground
From which a bare instant of cleavage or leg
Is all I shall have to sustain me. And yours
Are the text and the age I should like to be acting:
You lie on the bed of the lawn, painted gold,
With the base of your spine left naked to breathe,
And now I might seal the extravagant promise
To kiss you to life with your name, if for once
You could look at me – do it now – straight
In the eye, without smiling or shaking your head.

The Voice

Woman much missed, how you call to me, call to me,
Saying that now you are not as you were
When you had changed from the one who was all to me,
But as at first, when our day was fair.

Can it be you that I hear? Let me view you, then,
Standing as when I drew near to the town
Where you would wait for me: yes, as I knew you then,
Even to the original air-blue gown!

Or is it only the breeze, in its listlessness
Travelling across the wet mead to me here,
You being ever dissolved to wan wistlessness,
Heard no more again far or near?

    Thus I; faltering forward,
    Leaves around me falling,
Wind oozing thin through the thorn from norward,
    And the woman calling.

HUGO WILLIAMS

Bar Italia

How beautiful it would be to wait for you again
in the usual place,
not looking at the door,
keeping a lookout in the long mirror,
knowing that if you are late
it will not be too late,
knowing that all I have to do
is wait a little longer
and you will be pushing through the other customers,
out of breath, apologetic.
Where have you been, for God's sake?
I was starting to worry.

How long did we say we would wait
if one of us was held up?
It's been so long and still no sign of you.
As time goes by, I search other faces in the bar,
rearranging their features
until they are monstrous versions of you,
their heads wobbling from side to side
like heads on sticks.
Your absence inches forward
until it is standing next to me.
Now it has taken a seat I was saving.
Now we are face to face in the long mirror.

Index of First Lines

Here with a Loaf of Bread beneath the Bough, *40*
Hide the pink toothbrush, the dark nest of knickers. *88*
How beautiful it would be to wait for you again *165*
How do I love thee? Let me count the ways. *83*
How mild these young men seem to me now *128*

I knew a man who had a way with women. *86*
I leave myself about, slatternly, *145*
I ne'er was struck before that hour *2*
I wanted to be sure to reach you; *65*
I was never expected to sign the register *96*
I'd have walked straight past if you hadn't said *45*
If ever two were one, then surely we. *95*
If I were loved, as I desire to be, *17*
In the middle of the night, when we get up *5*
It might start with a wing-tip, snuck *30*
I've never held a gun, but knew *93*

John Anderson my jo, John, *32*

Lay your sleeping head, my love, *59*
Let me never have her father *18*
Let me not to the marriage of true minds *89*
Let us go then, you and I, *11*
'Let us not speak, for the love we bear one another— *55*
Look at this frosty red rose leaning over *162*
Love? Do I love? I walk *52*

Mark but this flea, and mark in this, *34*
Methought I saw my late espousèd Saint *99*
Miss J. Hunter Dunn, Miss J. Hunter Dunn, *7*
My heart is like a singing bird *4*
My mistress' eyes are nothing like the sun; *101*
My mouth blooms like a cut. *62*

Never the time and the place *105*
No matter what you did to her, she said, *143*
Not a red rose or a satin heart. *39*
Now sleeps the crimson petal, now the white; *142*

O my Luve's like a red, red rose, *38*
O rose, thou art sick! *70*
O verily you were readily forgot *100*
One day I wrote her name upon the strand, *20*
One word is too often profaned *87*
Out of the blackthorn edges *149*
Outside the cantina *25*

Passions never spoken, *90*

Seventeen years ago you said *81*
Shall I compare thee to a summer's day? *27*
She is all there. *109*
She pours down the phone at me, sobs, *155*
Shutters, broken, *35*
since feeling is first *3*
Since I noo mwore do zee your feäce, *134*
Since there's no help, come let us kiss and part; *144*
So, the year's done with! *84*
So, we'll go no more a-roving *78*
Some said, because he wud'n spaik *119*
somewhere i have never travelled,gladly beyond *82*
Spain frightened you. Spain *136*
Stop all the clocks, cut off the telephone, *106*
suck my red heart white, I will, because I love you, bless me, *33*
Sweet stream, that doth with equal pace *146*

Ten years since we were married, since we stood *139*
That time of year thou mayst in me behold *122*
The fountains mingle with the river *50*
The hunchèd camels of the night *42*
The night is fine and dry. It falls and spreads *41*
The shadows mediated by the slats of the venetian blind *21*
The storm shakes out its sheets *150*
They are not long, the weeping and the laughter, *154*
They flee from me that sometime did me seek, *117*
They were burning dead leaves. Must oozed with scent, *123*
This living hand, now warm and capable *56*

Index of Titles

Index of Poets

Acknowledgements

The publishers are grateful for permission to reproduce the following copyright material:

E. E. Cummings, 'since feeling is first': is reprinted from COMPLETE POEMS 1904–1962, by E. E. Cummings, edited by George J. Firmage, by permission of W.W. Norton & Company. Copyright © 1991 by the Trustees for the E.E. Cummings Trust and George James Firmage.

John Betjeman, 'A Subaltern's Love Song': from *Collected Poems*, by John Betjeman © The Estate of John Betjeman 1955, 1958, 1962, 1964, 1968, 1970, 1979, 1981, 1982, 2001. Reproduced by permission of John Murray (Publishers)

Roddy Lumsden, 'Prayer to be with Mercurial Women': from Roddy Lumsden, *Mischief Night: New & Selected Poems* (Bloodaxe Books, 2004)

Kate Clanchy, 'With Angels': from *Samarkand* (Picador, London, copyright © Kate Clanchy 1999)

John Glenday, 'Valentine': from *Grain* (Picador, London, copyright © John Glenday 2009)

Kathleen Jamie, 'The Swallows' Nest': from *The Tree House* (Picador, London, copyright © Kathleen Jamie 2004)

Glyn Maxwell, 'Stargazing': from *Boys at Twilight: Poems 1990–1995* (Bloodaxe Books, 2000)

Galway Kinnell, 'After Making Love We Hear Footsteps': from *Selected Poems* (Bloodaxe Books, 2001)

Carol Ann Duffy, 'Rapture': from *Rapture* (Picador, London, copyright © Carol Ann Duffy, 2005)

John Betjeman, 'In a Bath Tea Shop': from *Collected Poems*, by John Betjeman © The Estate of John Betjeman 1955, 1958, 1962, 1964, 1968, 1970, 1979, 1981, 1982, 2001. Reproduced by permission of John Murray (Publishers)

Michael Donaghy, 'The Present': from *Shibboleth* (Oxford University Press, 1988), repr. in *Collected Poems* (Picador, London, copyright © Michael Donaghy 2009)

W. H. Auden, 'Lullaby ('Lay your sleeping head, my love')': Copyright © 1976, The Estate of W.H. Auden

Hilaire Belloc, 'Tarantella': Extract from 'Tarantella' by Hilaire Belloc from *Sonnets and Verse* (© Hilaire Belloc, 1923) is reproduced by permission of PFD (www.pfd.co.uk) on behalf of The Estate of Hilaire Belloc.

E. E. Cummings, 'somewhere I have never travelled,gladly beyond': is reprinted from COMPLETE POEMS 1904–1962, by E. E. Cummings, edited by George J. Firmage, by permission of W.W. Norton & Company. Copyright © 1991 by the Trustees for the E.E. Cummings Trust and George James Firmage.

Annie Freud, 'Like What You Get When You Play It Backwards': from *The Best Man That Ever Was* (Picador, London, copyright © Annie Freud 2007)

Paul Farley, '*from* "Songs for Swingeing Lovers" ': from *The Boy from the Chemist is Here to See You* (Picador, London, copyright © Paul Farley 1998)

Colette Bryce, 'Nevers': from *The Heel of Bernadette* (Picador, London, copyright © 2000)

Sally Read, 'The Soldier's Girl': from *The Point of Splitting* (Bloodaxe Books, 2005)

Annie Freud, 'The Best Man That Ever Was': from *The Best Man That Ever Was* (Picador, London, copyright © Annie Freud 2007)

Lorraine Mariner, 'Second Wives': from *Furniture* (Picador, London, copyright © Lorraine Mariner 2009)

W. H. Auden, 'Funeral Blues ("Stop all the clocks")': copyright © 1991, The Estate of W.H. Auden

Michael Donaghy, 'Reprimands': from *Conjure* (Picador, London, copyright © Michael Donaghy 2000)

Lorraine Mariner, 'Feathers': from *Furniture* (Picador, London, copyright © Lorraine Mariner 2009)

Jake Polley, 'Sally Somewhere': from *Little Gods* (Picador, London, copyright © Jake Polley 2006)

Roddy Lumsden, 'Yeah Yeah Yeah'; from *Mischief Night: New & Selected Poems* (Bloodaxe Books, 2004)

Kate Clanchy, 'Slattern': from *Slattern* (Picador, London, copyright © Kate Clanchy 2001)

Robin Robertson, 'Static': from *A Painted Field* (Picador, London, copyright © Robin Robertson 1997)

Clive James, 'The Serpent Beguiled Me': from *Opal Sunset* (Picador, London, copyright © Clive James 2009)

Sean O'Brien, 'Indian Summer': from *Downriver* (Picador, London, copyright Sean O'Brien 2001)